T0368177

Hope Keepers Study Guide
for Families Caring *for* Mentally Ill Loved Ones

"Let us hold fast the confession of our hope without wavering, for He who promised is faithful." Hebrews 10:23 NKJV

JILL RUDOLPH RN, MSN, NP

WESTBOW
P R E S S®
A DIVISION OF THOMAS NELSON
& ZONDERVAN

Copyright © 2024 Jill Rudolph RN, MSN, NP.

All rights reserved. No part of this book may be used or reproduced by any means, graphic, electronic, or mechanical, including photocopying, recording, taping or by any information storage retrieval system without the written permission of the author except in the case of brief quotations embodied in critical articles and reviews.

This book is a work of non-fiction. Unless otherwise noted, the author and the publisher make no explicit guarantees as to the accuracy of the information contained in this book and in some cases, names of people and places have been altered to protect their privacy.

WestBow Press books may be ordered through booksellers or by contacting:

WestBow Press
A Division of Thomas Nelson & Zondervan
1663 Liberty Drive
Bloomington, IN 47403
www.westbowpress.com
844-714-3454

Because of the dynamic nature of the Internet, any web addresses or links contained in this book may have changed since publication and may no longer be valid. The views expressed in this work are solely those of the author and do not necessarily reflect the views of the publisher, and the publisher hereby disclaims any responsibility for them.

Any people depicted in stock imagery provided by Getty Images are models, and such images are being used for illustrative purposes only.
Certain stock imagery © Getty Images.

Unless otherwise indicated, All Scripture quotations marked (NKJV) are taken from the New King James Version. Copyright © 1982 by Thomas Nelson, Inc. Used by permission. All rights reserved.

Scripture quotations marked (NIV) are taken from the Holy Bible, NEW INTERNATIONAL VERSION®, NIV® Copyright © 1973, 1978, 1984, 2011 by Biblica, Inc.® Used by permission. All rights reserved worldwide.

Scripture quotations marked (NLT) are taken from the Holy Bible, New Living Translation, copyright © 1996, 2004, 2015 by Tyndale House Foundation. Used by permission of Tyndale House Publishers Inc., Carol Stream, Illinois 60188. All rights reserved.

ISBN: 979-8-3850-2927-3 (sc)
ISBN: 979-8-3850-2928-0 (e)

Library of Congress Control Number: 2024914288

Print information available on the last page.

WestBow Press rev. date: 08/15/2024

This Study Guide is dedicated to our daughter, Janae Christine Rudolph, who struggled with mental illness throughout most of her life. As a mother, having a child with mental illness was not on my radar. Our daughter was beautiful, loving, and full of laughter. But as she grew older into her teenage and young adult years, mental illness began to rob her of her joy. She struggled with ADHD, Bipolar Disorder, and Severe Anxiety. We tried everything we could think of to help her, and grieved as we watched our daughter slip away. I have known the pain and feeling of helplessness while caring for a loved one who is mentally ill. As a professional I have seen the impact of mental illness on adolescents and children. I worked as a school nurse/nurse practitioner for 36 years, and in later years I watched as mental illness became rampant among students. I provided care for countless students who struggled with Anxiety, Depression, Eating Disorders, Schizophrenia and Bipolar Disorder. I have counseled grieving parents who were at a loss as to how to meet their child's needs. I have seen the impact of mental illness both personally and professionally.

When I retired, I started praying for God to show me my next chapter. After much prayer and searching, He revealed to me that He wanted me to start a support group for families who are caring for loved ones with mental illness. There are very few support groups out there for families, especially faith-based ones. I also discovered that there were no published Study Guides for this type of support group. So, I stepped out in faith and asked God to guide me in not only starting a new ministry, but also in writing the Study Guide. The Support Group is called "Hope Keepers", and we are claiming Hebrews 10:23 NKJV, *"Let us hold fast the confession of our hope without wavering, for He who promised is faithful."* I believe that between both my personal journey and professional experience, I can provide information and guidance for others who are on this journey. The topics that are covered are ones that I have studied, experienced and learned from through God's Word and guidance. I pray this study guide will provide support, encouragement, and hope for families who are caring for mentally ill loved ones.

As I was writing the chapter on hope, on June 30, 2023, our daughter entered His kingdom and is now healed and fully restored. Her suffering has ended and her joy has returned. We are claiming that through her illness and suffering many people will be helped. What she couldn't do in life, God is using as a testimony in her death. To God be the glory who is our hope and anchor. Amen.

Resting in His Promises,
Jill

INTRODUCTION

Hope Keepers is a support group for those who have loved ones with Mental Illness. Our purpose is to encourage, support, and restore. We encourage by lifting one another up and provide a safe and confidential environment for sharing. We support through listening, prayer, showing love and compassion, and sharing resources. We restore by studying God's word and promises together, recognizing that we live in a fallen, broken world due to our sin. It is through His love and grace that we have hope, knowing He is the almighty healer.

Scripture Verse: Hebrews 10:23 NKJV, *"Let us hold fast the confession of our hope without wavering, for He who promised is faithful."*

Group Guidelines:

- Confidentiality is essential. We expect that each person will respect and maintain the confidentiality of the group.
- Be respectful of one another and recognize that everyone has their own personal experiences and insights. Try not to interrupt when another person is talking.
- Avoid crosstalk. Crosstalk is directing your comments to one person in the group rather than sharing your comments with the group as a whole.
- Please be sensitive to time while speaking so everyone can have opportunity to share.
- There is no requirement to share. Only participate with what is comfortable for you. It may take time to develop trust and feel comfortable.
- Please silence cell phones during the group meeting to avoid interruptions.
- Please try to be on time. It is understandable that situations happen with your loved one(s) that can delay you. The group will start on time and those who are delayed can join in when they arrive.

CONTENTS

CONTENTS

CHAPTER 1

Understanding the Root of Mental Illness

Why is this Happening?

The reality of sickness, death and dying originates from the sin of Adam and Eve in the Garden of Eden. God warned Adam and Eve of the consequence of being disobedient in Genesis 2:15-17 NKJV, *"Then the Lord God took the man and put him in the garden of Eden to tend and keep it. And the Lord God commanded the man, saying, 'Of every tree of the garden you may freely eat; but of the tree of the knowledge of good and evil you shall not eat, for in the day that you eat of it you shall surely die.'"* God told Adam and Eve that death would happen if they disobeyed Him, and sickness is part of that process. They chose to disobey God's command and ate the forbidden fruit. Since then, death, dying, and sickness have been the experience of humanity. Paul wrote about this truth in his letter to the Romans, and explained in Romans 5:12 NKJV, *"Therefore, just as through one man sin entered the world, and death through sin, and thus death spread to all men, because all sinned."*

Sickness and disease have been intertwined with sin and death since the fall of man. There was no sickness or pain in the Garden of Eden. Disease and death were a result of the disobedience of Adam and Eve, and entered into mankind the moment they left the garden. Science views the cause of diseases in physical and medical terms, whereas the Bible presents the underlining cause of sickness in spiritual terms. It was sin that brought death, sickness, and disease to the human race. As a result, we now use science and the knowledge that God has given us to treat and manage these diseases.

Now that we recognize that sin is the root cause of illness and disease and that we live in a fallen world, we need to understand mental illness and its impact on families. The American Psychiatric Association defines Mental Illness as health conditions that involve changes in emotion, thinking or behavior (or a combination of these). There are many different types of mental illness. Some of the main groups of mental disorders include:

- Mood disorders (such as depression or bipolar disorder)
- Anxiety disorders (including OCD)
- Personality disorders
- Psychotic disorders (such as schizophrenia)
- Eating Disorders
- Post Traumatic Stress Disorders (PTSD)
- Substance abuse disorders

Having a loved one with mental health issues can be very painful and traumatic. The emotional and behavioral toll on family members is often not recognized. It can be extremely stressful along with promoting physical, mental, and emotional consequences upon the family. Some of the issues that caretakers experience include, somatic problems (migraines, loss of appetite, fatigue, and insomnia), cognitive and emotional problems (anxiety, depression, guilt, fear, anger, confusion) and behavioral troubles (changes in attitude and social withdrawal). In addition, job attendance and performance can be impacted as well as having financial stressors.

Examples of common stressors that families encounter include:

- The child refuses to go to school or get out of bed due to anxiety/depression. They fall behind in school creating more stress and anxiety.
- The family member doesn't have access to care or refuses care.
- The family member is 18 years of age or older and the parent/caretaker no longer has input regarding their care.
- The family member refuses to take their medication and/or refuses help with managing their treatment/medication.
- The situation at home has become unsafe or overwhelming, impacting the family's quality of life.

Where Do I Go From Here?

Participating in a support group allows you to be with others who understand what you are going through and share a common understanding. Having a loved one with mental illness can be extremely stressful, exhausting, and draining. It is a trial that has no end date. It often feels like riding a roller coaster with many ups and downs, highs and lows. It can impact relationships within the family and marriages. It is a type of grief that keeps reoccurring, and the pain never seems to end.

Our journey started early in kindergarten when our daughter struggled with learning difficulties. Most of the teachers were supportive, but when we wanted her assessed for a learning disability, the school pushed back and refused. We ended up paying a private psychologist who specialized in learning disabilities to assess her. She was diagnosed with severe ADHD and a severe learning disability. We also had her assessed by a psychiatrist and she was started on medication for her ADHD. Her school performance and grades significantly improved, and we thought the worst was behind us. Later in high school her behaviors started to change, and she began experiencing severe anxiety. Unknown to us at that time, she was using alcohol and drugs to manage her symptoms. Her behavior became more erratic as she grew older, especially with anger, and she was eventually diagnosed with Bipolar Disorder. We tried everything we could think of to help her, but her actions and behaviors were affecting the family and our quality of life. Unfortunately, once she turned 18, we no longer had input regarding her treatment or medication management. She was not able to manage her medication and often ran out before the end of the month. She refused our help, and we could not communicate with the psychiatrist unless she gave permission.

This is a common issue for families caring for adult loved ones with mental illness. Their loved one struggles with managing their illness and they often end up depending on their family to care and provide for them. But the family has no input or control regarding their care and treatment. This takes a toll on families, and they often need to remove the adult from the home. This plays a large part in why the homeless population consists of many mentally ill people.

As you care for your loved one it is important to seek counsel from the Lord. He is your source of strength and comfort, and He promises that He will be with you through your struggles. He is your refuge as you endure trials and hardships. Meditate on the verses below.

"God is our refuge and strength, A very present help in trouble. Therefore we will not fear, Even though the earth be removed, And though the mountains be carried into the midst of the sea; Though its waters roar and be troubled, Though the mountains shake with its swelling." Psalm 46: 1-3, NKJV

"But now, thus says the Lord, who created you, O Jacob, And He who formed you, O Israel:' Fear not, for I have redeemed you; I have called you by your name; You are Mine. When you pass through the waters, I will be with you; And through the rivers, they shall not overflow you. When you walk through the fire, you shall not be burned, Nor shall the flame scorch you. For I am the Lord your God, The Holy One of Israel, your Savior;'" Isaiah 43: 1-3, NKJV

Place your hope and trust in our heavenly Father and learn to daily surrender your loved one to His care and control. No matter how hard you try you cannot control or fix them, you can only control yourself.

Below are some suggestions to help you cope as caregivers:

- Seek support from your family, friends, church, or join a support group.
- Research your loved one's diagnosis so you have a better understanding of their illness.
- Keep communication open with your loved one and try to understand their perspective. Take time to listen and try not to judge.
- Create healthy boundaries and learn the difference between helping and enabling.
- Balance your life with activities you enjoy. Be sure to make time for yourself.
- Implement strategies to help you manage stress. This can include prayer, practicing mindfulness, relaxation exercises, exercising regularly, and healthy eating.
- Have a plan in place for mental health emergencies. It is important to know who to call and how to contact a mental health facility.
- Encourage and support your loved one in receiving care and following through with the treatment recommendations.
- Learn how to express your frustration and anger in a constructive manner. Instead of being mad, realize that you are sad.
- Be realistic about your expectations and be willing to accept partial solutions. Focus your energy on what you can accomplish.

Reflection and Application

1. Do you believe that the cause of illnesses is due to our sin? Why or why not? How does this truth affect the way you view mental illness?

_____

_____

_____

_____

2. How do you feel about asking for or getting support? Who do you usually turn to, to help you cope? What are your expectations for participating in the support group?

_____

_____

_____

_____

3. What coping strategies can you use and apply? How will you implement them? Refer to the list provided or write out other strategies that you have used.

_____

_____

_____

_____

4. What are your goals for the future in relation to your mentally ill loved one?

_____

_____

_____

_____

Notes and Journaling

CHAPTER 2

Moving Beyond Grief

When we think about grief, it is usually for those who mourn the death of a loved one. Unlike the finality that comes with death, having a loved one with mental illness is a type of grief that has no end date. When someone dies at least their story has a definite end. With mental illness there is no sense of finality. We are grieving the loss of the loved one we knew before mental illness impacted them. We are grieving the loss of hopes, dreams, and a healthy relationship. We are grieving over the impact it is having on our lives and family. We are struggling because there is no sense of closure, and the pain is refreshed over, and over, again. It is stirred up with each crisis or negative encounter. This type of grief is referred to as "Ambiguous Grief" (grieving over someone who is still alive).

Ambiguous grief is a complicated grief in that the person is still alive and you have a strong sense of attachment to them. Even though there has been a dramatic shift in personality, you still love them and remember the person they once were. They are still very much a part of your life, but with that comes continuous pain and heartache.

Unlike grief over the death of a loved one, with ambiguous grief it is common to experience recurring negative emotions due to the continual impact of your loved one's illness. When a person dies, you are often surrounded by friends and family to comfort you. You share loving and joyful memories together. With ambiguous grief this rarely happens. People often do not know how to comfort you, or don't understand that you are grieving. Your sadness can intensify every time you think about or deal with your loved one. It is a grief that people cannot understand unless they have experienced a similar situation.

Ambiguous Grief and the Grief Process

Ambiguous grief is a complicated grief because you are often left longing for what the relationship used to be. There is no right or wrong way to grieve, but there are 5 common stages of grief:

- Denial
- Anger
- Bargaining
- Depression
- Acceptance

People who are grieving often go in and out of these stages in no particular order, and you can sometimes get stuck in any one stage. This is referred to as "frozen grief" or "grief limbo." It resembles ongoing trauma because there is no finality, and with each new crisis the grief process can begin all over again. It can feel like you are in an ongoing cycle with the different stages of grief, but never reaching acceptance. If you feel like you are stuck or experiencing grief limbo, there are some practical steps you can implement to help you move through the stages of grief.

The first step is to identify your loss(es) and the areas you are grieving over. Make a list of the losses you have experienced from your loved one's illness. For example, losses may include the loss of relationships, loss of hopes and dreams, loss of plans for the future, or loss of feeling safe. Write down the emotions you are experiencing from these losses and the stages of grief you are going through. Write out how each of these losses have impacted you and your family, and steps you can take to move forward and heal. Allow other family members to share their own grief experience and losses.

The next step is to identify the emotions you are experiencing, especially with anger and/or guilt. These emotions are a common response but can have a negative impact on you and your family. Keep a journal and write down the feelings and emotions you are having. Talk to someone you trust about your feelings and seek help when these emotions become overwhelming and unmanageable.

The third step is learning how to manage your thoughts and balance your thinking. Instead of focusing on absolutes, train you mind to re-direct your negative thinking. For example, when you think about your loved one tell yourself "They are no longer the person they used to be, but they are still alive and there is hope", or "I haven't been able to have closure with my losses, but I have the opportunity to move on with my life."

The fourth step is to develop strategies that will help you cope when you are feeling overwhelmed. This can include meditation, listening to music, reading, practicing mindfulness, exercising, or whatever calms you down. Having planned strategies in place will enable you to manage stressors, and prepare you for when those stressors become overwhelming.

Finally, seek support from trusted family, friends, church, and/or support groups. Don't try to manage it alone. Allow others to come along beside you to support you and your family in times of need. Also, keep communication open with your spouse and family. Allow open discussions to occur about your loved one, so everyone can express their concerns and participate in the solutions.

As you implement these steps, move towards renewing your hope for the future. Start making goals and plan activities for the future. Even in the midst of your grief, finding hope and seeking new opportunities will help you cope and give you a future to look forward to. Explore activities that interest you and look for new opportunities. This can include signing up for classes at a local community college, joining organized community groups through your church or local recreation center, or recruiting friends to join you for activities.

Jesus and Your Grief

We can obtain comfort and peace when grief seems to consume us. Jesus understands grief and was moved with compassion when Lazarus had died (read John 11:1-44). He reaches us when we are hurting, and ministers to us personally. He listens, guides, and when we weep, He remains with us and carries us. He demonstrated His compassion and understanding when He comforted Martha and Mary in this passage.

When you grieve, you may need to be comforted like Martha. She needed to be reminded of God's promises and stand on the truth of His word. While you are going through the journey of grief, spend time searching the scriptures to remind yourself of the countless times God provided hope and comfort to His people. Paul and the apostles experienced God's comfort through persecutions and imprisonment. David repeatedly wrote about God's comfort and promises in Psalms, such as Psalm 31:7 NLT, *"You have seen my troubles, and you care about the anguish of my soul."*

You may be the type of person who is like Mary who just needs to weep. You need to feel God's presence and the compassionate heart of Jesus, knowing that He personally experienced grief and sorrow. You gain comfort by crying out to God and pouring out your heart to Him. Cling to His promises and know that He hears you and cares about you. He sees your heartache and promises to wipe away every tear. He is your refuge and strength.

My husband and I have experienced both types of grief. We experienced ambiguous grief during the years we dealt with our daughter's illness, and then later the grief that came with her death. During her teenage and adult years, we repeatedly grieved as we watched her make bad choices, become angry and defiant, get into abusive relationships, use alcohol and drugs to manage her symptoms, do self-mutilating behaviors that left her with severe scars, and bounce between manic and depressive behaviors. We grieved over our loss of hopes and dreams for her future, and I personally grieved over the loss of having a close mother-daughter relationship. Our lives were always on edge waiting for the next phone call that presented a new crisis. We seemed to live in constant worry and pain. During this period, I was a "Martha" and needed the truth of God's word and His promises to bring me comfort. To help me I created a picture board that included photos of our daughter when she was young and full of innocence, before mental illness consumed her. I included scripture (Psalm 103:2-5) that I daily prayed and claimed over her. Later, when we lost her in death, I became a "Mary" and just needed to weep. I became numb and didn't know how to keep going. It was with the help of dear friends and family that I was able to move forward and heal. They allowed me to cry and share my pain, and God used them to remind me that He was present in my grief.

God's word encourages us and tells us that it is possible to grieve with hope. He promises to be with us in our sorrow, and even more so, He has made a way for us to find eternal hope in Christ Jesus. Because of this truth we can find hope in His promises, even in the deepest moments of our grief.

Below are some of His promises that you can claim as you grieve over your loved one.

- God promises to be near to you during your journey of grief: *"The Lord is near to those who have a broken heart, and saves such as have a contrite spirit."* Psalms 34:18 NKJV
- God encourages you to express your grief to Him through prayer: *"Have mercy on me, O Lord, for I am in trouble; My eye wastes away with grief, Yes, my soul and my body! For my life is spent with grief, and my years with sighing; My strength fails because of my iniquity, And my bones waste away."* Psalms 31:9-10 NKJV
- God promises to heal the brokenhearted from grief and sorrow: *"He heals the brokenhearted and binds up their wounds."* Psalms 147:3 NKJV
- God promises to use our deepest grief for good: *"And we know that all things work together for good to those who love God, to those who are called according to His purpose."* Romans 8:28 NKJV
- God promises that our grief is temporary: *"And God will wipe away every tear from their eyes; there shall be no more death, nor sorrow, nor crying. There shall be no more pain, for the former things have passed away."* Revelation 21:4 NKJV

Reflection and Application

1. What has been your grief experience? What specific things are you saddened by as you reflect on your relationship with your loved one?

_____

_____

_____

_____

2. What stage(s) of grief are you in right now? Do you feel like you are stuck in one of the stages? If so, are there one or more of the practical steps you can implement to help you move forward?

_____

_____

_____

_____

3. Do you feel like a Martha or a Mary or maybe both? How does their example help you to move forward in your grief?

_____

_____

_____

_____

4. Which promise in God's word encourages you and gives you hope? You may want to memorize a verse(s) to go to when you need His reassurance.

_____

_____

_____

_____

Notes and Journaling

CHAPTER 3

Facing Our Fears

Fear Over Our Loved Ones

Fear is a common emotion experienced by families caring for a mentally ill loved one, and there are many ways fear can be manifested. For example, you may fear that your loved one or you yourself will be judged by others. Or you may fear that your child will be picked on or bullied at school. You may fear about their future and worry if they will be able to obtain a job, maintain relationships, take care of their needs, and/or live independently. You may fear that they may harm themselves or others. Or fear that you will make wrong decisions regarding their care or treatment. As you age you may fear about what will happen to them when you are gone. These are all common fears and understandable.

As a caregiver, you may fear for your own personal quality of life and future. Caring for a mentally ill family member is a huge responsibility, and it is normal to fear for your own well-being. This is especially true if your loved one is aggressive or unstable. Having a mentally ill loved one is a major life change, and the future you once envisioned for yourself has significantly changed. It is understandable that you fear over what your own personal future will look like. You may ask yourself if you ever will be able to enjoy life without stress and worry? Will you be able to cope?

How will your later years be impacted? Caring for a mentally ill person creates a lot of unknowns, and it is understandable if you experience fear over the unpredictable. All these fears are very real and justified. The challenge is keeping these fears from consuming and overwhelming you.

Anticipatory Fear

Anticipatory fear is a form of worry or anxiety that occurs when you continually worry about the future. You find yourself constantly thinking about bad things that may happen, and/or feel out of control over potential situations. Although these feelings are normal, they can intensify over time and impact your quality of life. Feelings can range from temporary nervousness to an overwhelming feeling of dread. Constantly thinking about worst-case scenarios may lead to increased anxiety and worry, which can eventually take a toll on your well-being.

Experiencing chronic anticipatory fear can impact your physical and emotional health. Examples of physical side effects include muscle tension and pain, difficulty concentrating, increase or decrease in appetite, or difficulty sleeping. Emotional side effects can include restlessness, irritability, mood swings, emotional numbness, or having an overwhelming sense of impending doom. Over time, anticipatory fear can impact your mental health and may eventually lead to chronic anxiety or Generalized Anxiety Disorder.

There are other potential outcomes from anticipatory fear, such as becoming obsessive over managing your loved one's life. You believe that if you micromanage their lives, you will be able to protect them and control their future. But this often leads to frustration and increased fear, especially if your loved one pushes back or fails to meet your expectations. It is normal to want to control the future, but the truth is, no one can because life is an uncertain journey. No matter how hard we try, we cannot always be there to protect our loved ones from harm or bad choices.

Another possible outcome or response to anticipatory fear is avoidance. This includes avoiding social or family gatherings because you worry that you will be questioned about your loved one, or your loved one will act out. Or avoiding school events because your child might stand out or other parents may make comments. It may even include not attending church because you fear you will be judged or criticized. These are valid fears, and it is understandable that you may want to avoid these situations.

Managing Anticipatory Fear

Experiencing Anxiety about something that may occur in the future is the most common symptom of anticipatory fear. If you struggle with constant worry, below are some practical strategies you can apply to help manage the symptoms.

- Practice mindfulness. The purpose of mindfulness is to help you redirect your thoughts back to the present. To accomplish this, you need to distance yourself from anxious thoughts by looking at them objectively. Are your fears valid? Can you truly control the outcome? Realize that your thoughts only have as much control as you are willing to give them.

- Perform relaxation exercises such as belly breathing. This is done by the following steps:

  - Get into a comfortable position by either sitting or laying down.
  - Place your hands on your chest and abdomen.
  - Slowly breathe in through your nose and out through your mouth. You may want to count to 5 with each breath in, and then again as you exhale. Make sure your belly is rising and falling, and your chest is remaining still.
  - Continue this for 5 minutes or until you feel relaxed.

- Write your worries in a Journal. When you write down your thoughts and feelings, it can help put things in perspective. It allows you to organize your thoughts and develop an awareness of patterns. It can bring clarity and allow you to come up coping strategies.
- Practice positive thinking. Instead of focusing on the negative, start looking at potential positive outcomes. Work on changing your thought processes so that you can see the good that can come out of bad or hard situations. It may be something as simple as "I am becoming more patient." You may benefit from writing down your positive affirmations in a journal to remind you of the progress you have made.
- Talk to trusted family members or friends. Sharing your anxieties with loved ones can help provide reassurance and comfort. They can help you to put things in perspective and come up with ways to manage.

What the Bible Says About Fear

God understands our fears, so much so that He gave us 365 verses in the Bible about fear. One for every day of the year. He knows that we will experience fear and anxiety, that is why He warned us that we live in a world where we will have tribulation. In Scripture, God addresses both rational fears (actual threats to our safety or well-being) and irrational fears (worries over what might happen). When referring to irrational fear the Bible describes it as having a "spirit of fear." It is a mindset that is focused on potential harm and a belief that something bad is going to happen. When we live in fear though, we are showing a lack of trust in God. Satan, the father of lies, works hard to instill fear into us. But God wants us to rest in Him. He has given us ammunition to overcome fear in His word and repeatedly tells us "Do not be afraid!"

Jesus tells us in Matthew 6:34 NKJV, *"Therefore do not worry about tomorrow, for tomorrow will worry about its own things. Sufficient for the day is its own trouble."* Our anxiety comes from uncertainty of the future. When we worry, we are doubting our sovereign God and not trusting that He is in control. Worry hijacks our minds into focusing on tomorrow, filling us with doubts and details we cannot control. When we focus on tomorrow, we miss the blessings of today.

The way to overcome our fear starts with trusting God. He has not abandoned us, and when we are in the storms of life we are continually under His watchful eye. His active care is always present. He wants us to trust Him and rely on Him for everything, including the future. God knows what the future holds because He has promised that He has already gone before us. He tells us in Deuteronomy 31:8 NKJV, *"And the Lord, He is the One who goes before you. He will be with you, He will not leave you nor forsake you; do not fear nor be dismayed."*

How to Trust God with The Future

It is easy to say that you will trust God, but putting that into practice can be very difficult. There are truths you need to know to help strengthen your faith. Believing in these truths will help you to confidently put your trust in God for the future.

The first truth is that God is sovereign. He is omniscient (all-knowing), omnipotent (all-powerful), and omnipresent (in all places). He knows the past, present, and future. When you worry about the future, remember that He already knows it, has been there, and will never leave you. That doesn't mean that He won't allow bad things to happen, but He promises to walk with us through the trials. He only allows hardships in our life because of the good He promises to bring out of them. He uses trials to bring us closer to Him, deepen our faith, and strengthen our character.

The next truth is that God loves us, wants the best for us, and promises to take care of us. He loved us enough to send His son to die for us and pay the price for our sins. He shows His love by guiding us, strengthening us, and protecting us today and tomorrow. Read Matthew 26: 25-34. In this passage Jesus reminds us that God takes care of the birds of the air and the lilies of the field; how much more so will He take care of us.

God has also given us the truth that His plans are above our plans. He is the Master at work, weaving everything together. He is the potter, and we are the clay. We need to trust that His plans are much greater than anything we can anticipate. He sees the overall beautiful painting when we can only see the brush strokes. He tells us in Isaiah 55: 8-9 NKJV, *"For My thoughts are not your thoughts, Nor are your ways My ways," says the Lord. 'For as the heavens are higher than the earth, So are My ways higher than your ways, And My thoughts than your thoughts.'"*

We also have the truth that God gives us grace. He gives us grace to face whatever the future holds, especially during times of hardship and difficulty. He doesn't want us dwelling on the "what-ifs," because He has promised to equip us with everything we need to persevere through trials.

Finally, we have the truth that when we are obedient to His word, He will bless us. As we obediently walk in His ways, He guides us step by step and is our solid foundation. He promises in Matthew 7:24 NKJV, *"Therefore whoever hears these sayings of Mine, and does them, I will liken him to a wise man who built his house on the rock: and the rain descended, the floods came, and the winds blew and beat on that house; and it did not fall, for it was founded on the rock."*

As we learn to trust and surrender the future to God, we will receive His peace that surpasses all understanding. Meditate on the following scriptures and claim one or more of them to help you manage your fear.

Scripture to Overcome Fear

"Have I not commanded you? Be strong and of good courage; do not be afraid, nor be dismayed, for the Lord your God is with you wherever you go." Joshua 1:9 NKJV

"For God has not given us a spirit of fear, but of power and of love and of a sound mind." 2 Timothy 1:7 NKJV

"Fear not, for I am with you; Be not dismayed, for I am your God. I will strengthen you, Yes, I will help you, I will uphold you with My righteous right hand." Isaiah 41:10 NKJK

Reflection and Application

1. Are you experiencing anticipatory fears over your loved one? What are some of those fears?

_____

_____

_____

_____

2. Are you willing or able to apply any of the practical strategies to help you with managing your fears and anxiety? If so, which ones?

_____

_____

_____

_____

3. Are you struggling with trusting God with both your future and the future of your loved one? Which of the truths can you focus on to help you with developing trust?

_____

_____

_____

_____

4. Did any of the scripture verses speak to you about coping with fear? Write them down and meditate on them daily.

_____

_____

_____

_____

Notes and Journaling

CHAPTER 4

Power of Forgiveness

Forgiving Our Loved One

Having a loved one with mental illness is exhausting, painful, and can be traumatizing. Their behaviors can include self-harm, verbal abuse, emotional abuse, and sometimes physical abuse. We need to remember that mental illness is not a choice, and many times beyond their control. It is a disease that can consume both the individual and the family trying to help them. It can create feelings of anger, resentment, embarrassment, and shame within the family. Oftentimes, the stress of living with and caring for a family member who is mentally ill, can put a strain on family relationships. Separation and divorce are not uncommon in families who are struggling with mental illness. Children and siblings of a mentally ill family member are also impacted and can be confused or fearful of their behaviors. Sometimes siblings can be resentful of the other sibling who requires a lot of time and attention from the parents.

Growing up or living with family member(s) who are mentally ill can cause unresolved feelings of anger, resentment, guilt, helplessness, and depression. Oftentimes we carry these feelings with us for years and into adulthood. We hang on to the memories, which can lead to bitterness and resentment. It can impact our other relationships because we have unresolved hurt and pain.

This is where forgiveness plays a vital role in our healing and recovery. It is important to not hang on to the past hurts or the damage our ill family members have caused. We need to let go of this burden and allow God's healing to take place in our lives. We may never forget the pain and hurt, but we can be restored by His healing grace through forgiveness.

Forgiveness has the power and ability to transform lives and heal broken relationships. As Christians, we are commanded to forgive others who have hurt us, just as God has forgiven us. God doesn't expect us to just forget about our hurt, His forgiveness goes much deeper than that. It means that we are to let go of our hurt and anger, and replace it with showing love and mercy to the person who has hurt us. We forgive because God has forgiven us, not because the other person deserves it. None of us deserves to be forgiven, but we receive His grace and forgiveness because of what Christ did on the cross.

God's ultimate example of forgiveness is found in His love for us. Even though mankind has repeatedly sinned and rebelled, He sent His son to die on the cross so that we can obtain His grace and mercy. As believers we are called to follow His example and forgive others who have wronged us. This goes against our human nature and is difficult for most of us. But when we rely on His strength and grace, we can forgive and obtain the freedom that comes with it.

Forgiveness is powerful because it can bring healing and restoration to relationships. When we extend forgiveness to someone, we are releasing them from the debt they owe us and allowing the door of reconciliation to be opened. It is important to realize though that forgiveness does not require an apology, and the other person may never admit to their wrongdoing. Regardless, we are called to forgive not just for the other person's benefit, but especially for our own. When we forgive, we are releasing the weight that comes with carrying resentment and anger. It releases the burden of bitterness and allows us to live in joy and freedom. It allows us to move forward with a clear conscience.

Forgiving Ourselves

As parents or caregivers for mentally ill family members, we often experience feelings of guilt or inadequacy. We believe we should have or could have done something more for our loved one. Sometimes we blame ourselves for not providing good enough care. For example, we may tell ourselves "I should have recognized her symptoms sooner," or "I should have gotten better doctors or therapists," or "I should have pushed harder for the schools to assess her." It is easy to blame ourselves and feel guilty about our loved one's illness.

Below are some common feelings caregivers experience and examples of caregiver guilt.

- Frustration with our loved one. It is easy to lose your temper when you are frustrated and exhausted. We feel guilty when we do this and often blame ourselves.
- Resentment over the amount of time and energy they take from you. It's normal to feel resentment over their impact on your life and all you've had to give up because of them. But this can cause feelings of guilt because you are feeling resentful.

- Feeling inadequate. You may feel guilty that you are not doing a good job caring for your loved one and managing their issues.
- Asking for help. We want to believe that we can do it all, but eventually it will lead to exhaustion and burnout. You may feel guilt because you believe you are inept or a failure if you need help.
- Conflict or unresolved issues. Family dynamics can be greatly impacted, and conflict can escalate from the stress of caring for a loved one. Guilt can come from unresolved past issues or blame.
- Taking time to care for your own needs. Guilt can come from taking time for yourself. We feel we are being selfish and that our loved one's needs are more important than our own.

Coping with Caregiver guilt

Caregiver guilt can have a significant impact on the mental and emotional well-being of caregivers, and can lead to depression, anxiety, and burnout. It is important for caregivers to recognize and address these feelings to maintain their own health and well-being. There are strategies you can implement to help manage and prevent caregiver guilt:

- Practice self-care: Caregivers should prioritize their own physical and mental health needs, taking time to engage in activities that bring them joy and relaxation.
- Seek support: Caregivers should ask for support from friends, family, and other caregivers who can provide empathy and understanding.
- Address negative self-talk: Caregivers need to be aware of negative self-talk and remind themselves that they are doing the best they can in a difficult situation.
- Find ways to cope: Caregivers should explore different coping strategies, such as meditation, journaling, exercising, or talking to a therapist to help manage the stress and anxiety.
- Set realistic expectations: Caregivers should set realistic expectations for themselves and their loved one, recognizing that they may not be able to do everything and that it is okay to ask for help.

Ultimately, caregivers need to remember that feeling guilty is a natural part of caregiving and it does not diminish the love and care they are providing for their loved one. By taking care of their own needs and seeking support, caregivers can better manage their feelings of guilt and maintain their own well-being.

What The Bible Tells Us About Guilt

God has provided us freedom from guilt and offers us His love and compassion. We have been freed from condemnation as believers in Christ Jesus (Romans 8:1-2). Just as God has forgiven and extended His grace to us, we need to extend grace to ourselves.

In this world we need to remember that we are in a spiritual warfare. Satan is the father of lies and hates truth (John 8:44). He is described as our adversary who *"prowls around like a roaring lion seeking someone to devour"* (1 Peter 5:8 NIV). He attacks us at our weakest points, which includes our feelings of guilt. Ephesians 6:12 NKJV tells us *"...we do not wrestle against flesh and blood, but against principalities, against powers, against the rulers of the darkness of this age, against spiritual hosts of wickedness in the heavenly places."* As we go through our day-to-day struggles, remember that even though we feel like we are losing the battle, Jesus has already won the war. He conquered death and sin on the cross. Satan has no power or authority over us because we are children of the Savior, the true Living God.

Scripture Verses on Forgiveness:

"And be kind to one another, tenderhearted, forgiving one another, even as God in Christ forgave you." Ephesians 4:32, NKJV

"Therefore, as the elect of God, holy and beloved, put on tender mercies, kindness, humility, meekness, longsuffering; bearing with one another, and forgiving one another, if anyone has a complaint against another; even as Christ forgave you, so you also must do." Colossians 3:12-13, NKJV

"For You, Lord, are good, and ready to forgive, and abundant in mercy to all those who call upon You." Psalm 86:5, NKJV

Reflection and Application

1. How has your loved one's illness/behaviors impacted you and/or your family? Have you been able to forgive past hurts and pain?

_____

_____

_____

_____

2. Are you experiencing Caregiver guilt? In what areas? Are they justified or self- applied?

_____

_____

_____

_____

3. Have you struggled with guilt and blame/shame? Which of the listed coping strategies for caregivers can you use or apply?

_____

_____

_____

_____

4. Do you believe that God has forgiven us of all guilt and shame? Do you believe that we are in a spiritual warfare? What does scripture say about our spiritual battles (read Ephesians 6:10-20)?

_____

_____

_____

_____

Notes and Journaling

Control vs Surrender

Why We Want Control

Having a loved one who suffers from mental illness is difficult and challenging. It is hard being around them and watching them struggle and suffer. We want to protect them and make everything alright. It is a common and natural response to want to take control or remain in control of their lives. We are naturally inclined to want to control their treatment, medication, life choices, getting or keeping jobs, and relationships. Oftentimes the loved one may push back, and the more you try to take control the more they tend to withdraw or resist your efforts. This is especially difficult when we know they need treatment, but they refuse to participate or follow the treatment plan. As caretakers, whether we are the parent, spouse, sibling, or child, it is exhausting trying to control and manage their lives.

A common feeling caregivers have is fear. We may fear our loved one may be harmed or harm themselves, or fear they won't get the right treatment or manage their medication, or fear they will not be able to get or keep a job, or fear for their future (what will happen when I'm not here?). This is the catalyst that makes us want to take control to protect them. We think that if we control their world, maybe no harm will come to them. We believe that they are not able to manage their lives by themselves.

Another cause for taking control may be due to a lack of resources. There may be financial obstacles as we try to find the care that they need. Oftentimes insurance requires a percentage or high deductible to cover the cost. Many families become overwhelmed by finances and lack of resources. We take control to manage some of the financial burdens and find affordable care.

Sometimes, we as caregivers place unreasonable burdens upon ourselves. We believe that providing care is our exclusive responsibility. Family members such as siblings, adult children, or the mentally ill loved one themselves may place unreasonable demands on the caregiver and disregard their own responsibilities. The expectation is that the caregiver will continue to maintain control to keep the peace within the home and family.

With our daughter, I was the primary caretaker and managed her treatment plan. Over time my control expanded, and I was managing most of her life such as finding a job, doing her taxes, ordering her medication, you name it, and I did it! I believed she was incapable of doing these things. The problem was that she became more dependent on me and was fearful of doing them herself. As she got older, I realized I had to let go of my control and allow her to assume responsibility for her own affairs. It was difficult, especially when she would panic and act like she was incapable of doing things on her own. It was a gradual process, but eventually she took on more responsibility and became less dependent on me. She often made bad decisions, especially with finances, and she expected me to fix them. I had to accept that she was an adult and was responsible for her life. I had to reconcile that she may even end up homeless. It was a brutal realization, but gradually I learned to let go and surrender her to the Lord. It was a day-to-day struggle and daily surrendering.

God's Perspective on Our Control

Whatever the reason for us controlling our loved one's care, it is a burden that can impact our own well-being. We can become so focused on their needs, that we neglect our own emotional, physical, and spiritual health. The demands placed on us as caregivers can leave us feeling overwhelmed, exhausted, depressed and hopeless. God does not want us to carry our loved one's burdens. He tells us in Psalm 55:22 NKJV, *"Cast your burden on the Lord, And He shall sustain you; He shall never permit the righteous to be moved."*

Letting go of control is not easy. We may want to release our control to God, but our fear and uncertainty hinders us. We don't like it if we can't control or foresee the outcome. The truth is that we don't have control over our loved one. The enemy instills fear, worry, and doubt in our minds, leading us to believe we need to rely on our own strength and wisdom. Releasing control to the Lord means allowing Him to take it completely from us. It is an active, conscious choice to surrender the things we cannot control. As we hand over our control to the Lord, we will experience the peace that passes all understanding and we can rest in His promises.

It is important to recognize that the only person in control of anything is God. Proverbs 19:21 NIV tells us, *"Many are the plans in a person's heart, but it is the Lord's purpose that prevails."*

It is during those times when everything seems like it is spinning out of control, that we finally surrender our control over to God. It's as if He says, "finally, now will you let me do it." His ways are always infinitely better that our ways, and He can restore order to the chaos we have created. When we surrender, we are filled with His peace.

We also need to understand that control is the enemy of rest. The energy we expend trying to manage and control everything can lead to exhaustion. Jesus tells us in Matthew 11:28 NKJV, *"Come to me, all you labor and are heavy laden and I will give you rest."* Our nature is to want to hold on tighter and grip harder. Jesus tells us to come to Him and release our burdens to Him. He wants us to let go of our hold and allow Him to be our rest.

Blessings of Surrendering

This leads us to the why and how of surrendering our loved one to the Lord. The "why" is because surrendering to the Lord gives us freedom from our worries. It allows Him to take our yoke upon Him and carry our burdens. When we surrender and give our loved one over to Jesus, it allows Him to do the heavy lifting. It allows Him to produce the heart change, perform the miracles, and transform your loved one into the person He made him or her to be.

The "how" of surrendering requires a complete trust in God. It means getting out of the driver's seat and allowing God to drive. It requires a daily letting go of your loved one and prayerfully laying them at the altar of His feet. It is saying out loud, "I release them to your care." It means that you believe and understand that God loves your loved one even more than you do, and He wants the best for them. It is trusting that He will never take His hand off them, and whatever the future holds, His ways are perfect.

It is hard to surrender. We want to hold tightly onto our loved one and believe that it is our responsibility to protect them. To help you take this step of faith, here are some practical steps you can implement to help you in surrendering:

- First, focus on God and recognize Him for who He is. He is the Creator, maker of heaven and earth, who knew us before we were born and knit us together in the womb. God always has and always will be sovereign and in control. He is a loving Heavenly Father who cares about our every need.
  His word encourages us:

  Psalm 121:1-2 NKJV, *"I will lift up my eyes to the hills— From whence comes my help? My help comes from the Lord, Who made heaven and earth."*

  Psalm 139:13 NKJV *"For you formed my inward parts; you covered me in my mother's womb."*

- Next, pray daily for your loved one and ask for God's protection over them. No matter how hard we try we cannot protect those we love from harm, whether they are mentally ill or not. Take time to read and meditate on Psalm 91.
- Finally, trust God. We need to have faith that He will keep His promises and do what He says He will do. On those days when you struggle or are burdened, remind yourself of His unfailing love. Trust in our loving God and lay your loved one at His feet. Place them on His altar for redemption and healing.

*Remember these three simple steps: Focus, Pray, and Trust.

Scripture for Surrendering

"Peace I leave with you, My peace I give to you; not as the world gives do I give to you. Let not your heart be troubled, neither let it be afraid." John 14:27, NKJV

"I sought the LORD, and He heard me, and delivered me from all my fears." Psalm 34:4, NKJV

"Trust in the Lord with all your heart, and lean not on your own understanding; In all your ways acknowledge Him, and He shall direct your paths." Proverbs 3:5-6 NKJV

"And those who know Your name will put their trust in You; For You, Lord, have not forsaken those who seek You." Psalms 9:10 NKJV

Reflection and Application

1. Are you struggling with control? What areas of your loved one's life are you trying to manage?

_____

_____

_____

_____

2. What are some areas you struggle with relinquishing control? How is this impacting your physical, emotional, and spiritual health?

_____

_____

_____

_____

3. When you think of surrendering your loved one to the Lord, do you have peace or more worry and anxiety? Are you able to apply the steps (focus, pray, trust)?

_____

_____

_____

_____

4. Reflect on the verses listed. Which ones speak to you the most and why?

_____

_____

_____

_____

Notes and Journaling

CHAPTER 6

Enable or Empower

Recognize Enabling

Enabling can often be confused with what we think is supporting or helping our loved one. It can become a blurred boundary that crosses over into doing for a loved one what they can and should do for themselves. When we are in the trenches trying to live with or support our mentally ill loved one, it can be very difficult to tell the difference between supporting and enabling.

To understand the difference between supporting or enabling, we need to look at the progress or changes our loved one is making. We may believe we are providing healthy support, but in truth we are enabling them to continue their behavior patterns. Examples include giving them money, making excuses or covering for them, or ignoring their behaviors to avoid conflict. Oftentimes we start out by just trying to help them, but over time our help can lead to reinforcing their behaviors.

Our daughter struggled with money management, especially impulsive spending. She would repeatedly call for help with a financial crisis, desperate for money. Each time I helped her and bailed her out, she promised she would do better and not let it happen again. As you can guess, it was only a matter of time before she was back in a financial predicament. I allowed her to manipulate my emotions and felt I needed to help her. It took confrontation by family and friends for me to acknowledge and accept that I was enabling her to fail. She knew that I would bail her out with the next crisis. It was difficult for me to say no to her, and I had to continually remind myself that my actions were preventing her from growing and becoming responsible.

Signs of enabling may include:

- Making excuses for their unhealthy behaviors. We want to protect them or justify their behaviors because they are struggling or going through a difficult time.
- Taking on more of their responsibilities. This can include doing their chores or homework, managing their bills and bank accounts, or paying for their needs (housing, food, clothing, etc.). As we continue to allow them to rely on us, they become less motivated to handle their own responsibilities.
- Trying to solve their problems for them. This can be financial, job issues, interpersonal relationships, legal issues, etc.
- Avoiding conflict. We may be hesitant to set boundaries, which can reinforce the unhealthy behavior(s). Fear of their reaction can keep us from setting and enforcing healthy boundaries.
- Ongoing financial support. Lending occasional financial support to loved ones is not uncommon. However, if you are continually covering for poor financial choices and bailing them out, this is a sign of having enabling behaviors.
- Experiencing resentment. As we invest our time and energy managing our loved one's responsibilities, we may feel unappreciated for our work. We may struggle with being exhausted and resentful due to our inability to stop our enabling actions.
- Ignoring our own needs. We put our loved one's needs before our own which can impact our emotional, physical, and spiritual health.

It is important to recognize when your support has crossed over into an enabling (also called a codependent) relationship. Sometimes we need to seek input from trusted family and friends to see things more clearly. It may be difficult, but it is possible to change your patterns back to healthy ones for both you and your loved one.

If you are struggling with limiting or stopping your enabling behaviors, there are some steps you can implement to help you do this. First, you need to separate yourself from the behaviors of your loved one, not your loved one themselves. Let them know that you love them but are no longer going to take responsibility for the things they should be doing themselves. Step back and allow them to face the consequences of their behaviors (financial, relationships, work, etc.). This includes separating yourself from their fallout, which is difficult. They are used to running to you when consequences happen, and they will try to manipulate your emotions into rescuing them. Stay committed to changing your enabling behaviors and ask for support from family and friends if needed.

Next, create and set boundaries. You need to clarify what behaviors you will no longer tolerate, what your limits are, and how you want to be treated. For example, you decide that you are no longer going to bail them out when they make poor financial decisions, or you are no longer going call their boss and make excuses for them when they don't show up to work. It is important to stick with the boundaries you have set so your loved one knows you are serious. It will be difficult, especially as you see them struggle, but eventually they will realize that they need to manage their own responsibilities.

It is important to seek support from family and friends if you feel you are unable to stop enabling your loved one. They can help you to see the clear picture and understand how your behaviors are hindering your loved one. Ask them to keep you accountable and help you stand firm with maintaining the boundaries. You will need their support as you face possible opposition.

Finally, take time to focus on your own health and needs. Taking care of yourself is not being selfish. It is important to invest in your own physical, emotional, and spiritual health, which will strengthen your mind, body, and soul. When you are healthy, you are better able to manage the stresses of caring for you loved one.

Understanding God's Perspective on Enabling

It is sometimes hard to see the difference between helping and enabling. As Christians we are taught to love and help one another, but God discourages enabling one another. 2 Thessalonians 3:10-11 NKJV says, *"For even when we were with you, we commanded you this: If anyone will not work, neither shall he eat. For we hear that there are some who walk among you in a disorderly manner, not working at all, but are busybodies."* God allows us to suffer the consequences of poor choices and tells us to not support bad behaviors. This doesn't mean that He doesn't love us or want the best for us, but He does want us to learn from our mistakes.

It is normal to want the best for our loved ones and protect them from making bad choices. But if we want them to become self-sufficient, we need to allow them to face the consequences of their choices. One of the best examples of this is the story of the prodigal son (read Luke 15: 11-32). In this story, the son went to his father and demanded his part of the inheritance so he could leave and live the way he chose. It was painful for the father to see his son make that choice, but he realized he needed to let his son go and face the consequences of his decision. Eventually the son spent all the money and hit bottom. In the depth of his despair, he realized he had been wrong and returned home with a repentant heart. His father welcomed him home with open arms and never stopped caring for him. It was hard, but his father realized that he needed to allow God to discipline him. To have a lasting change in behavior, we need to allow God to do His work in our loved one so they can have a lasting change in their heart and mind.

It is natural for us to want to avoid suffering, and it is especially difficult to watch our loved ones suffer. But suffering from consequences is not a bad thing. When we intervene, we are keeping them from experiencing the power of God's forgiveness, grace, and mercy. He tells us in Hebrews 12:11 NKJV, *"Now no chastening seems to be joyful for the present, but painful; nevertheless, afterward it yields the peaceable fruit of righteousness to those who have been trained by it."* When we step back and allow our loved one to face the consequences of their choices, we are partnering with God and helping to free them from the power of sin.

Empowering Our Loved One

When we empower our loved one, we assist and guide them with managing their illness and responsibilities. We do not do it for them, instead we build them up and help them to gain a sense of control over their lives. We help them to develop confidence and a sense of autonomy. The difficult part is figuring out how to move from enabling to empowering. This is where we need to completely surrender our control and allow God to empower us and our loved ones.

Jesus demonstrated how to empower when He sent the disciples out in pairs to minister to people. Mark 6:7-9,12 NKJV, *"And He called the twelve to Himself, and began to send them out two by two, and gave them power over unclean spirits. He commanded them to take nothing for the journey except a staff—no bag, no bread, no copper in their money belts— but to wear sandals, and not to put on two tunics...So they went out and preached that people should repent. And they cast out many demons, and anointed with oil many who were sick, and healed them."* Jesus empowered them to take responsibility and control over their situations. He provided them with the opportunity to learn, make mistakes, and have successes and failures. He pushed them to take responsibility for their own ministry, ultimately preparing them for when He would no longer be there to guide them.

As believers in the Lord Jesus Christ, we are empowered by God through the Holy Spirit. We need to teach this truth to our loved ones and show them how to embrace this empowerment. They will experience fear as we have them take on responsibility, but with our encouragement and reminder of God's love for them, they can be strengthened and gain empowerment. Share with them scriptures of God's promise to never leave us. Have your loved one choose either one or more of the verses listed, or search for other verses that give them encouragement. Post them on the mirror or where they can be seen to remind them of God's promises.

Scripture on Empowerment:

"Be strong and of good courage, do not fear nor be afraid of them; for the Lord your God, He is the One who goes with you. He will not leave you nor forsake you." Deuteronomy 31:6 NKJV

"Fear not, for I am with you; Be not dismayed, for I am your God. I will strengthen you, Yes, I will help you, I will uphold you with My righteous right hand." Isaiah 41:10 NKJV

"But those who wait on the Lord Shall renew their strength; They shall mount up with wings like eagles, They shall run and not be weary, They shall walk and not faint." Isaiah 40:31 NKJV

"When you pass through the waters, I will be with you; And through the rivers, they shall not overflow you. When you walk through the fire, you shall not be burned, Nor shall the flame scorch you." Isaiah 43:2 NKJK

Reflection and Application

1. Do you struggle with enabling your mentally ill loved one? What areas are you enabling them? If you aren't sure, discuss this with a trusted family member or friend.

_____

_____

_____

_____

2. What steps can you implement to help you with changing your enabling habits over to healthy supportive behaviors?

_____

_____

_____

_____

3. What is your understanding of God's perspective on enabling? Are there areas that you struggle with?

_____

_____

_____

_____

4. How do you feel about empowering your loved one? Read Matthew 10:1-20. What way did Jesus empower them? How can you apply His example?

_____

_____

_____

_____

Notes and Journaling

CHAPTER 7

Boundaries

Understanding Boundaries

We are often told or have read about the importance of setting boundaries. Boundaries are a way to protect ourselves by setting clear guidelines on how we want to be treated. It lets others know what is acceptable and what is not. Setting boundaries is a form of self-care that honors our need to feel safe and respected.

There are several types of boundaries that can be identified:

- <u>Physical boundaries</u>: refers to your personal space and/or physical contact. This includes respecting your personal space (such as your bedroom) and setting limits on who and when they can enter that space. It also includes boundaries with physical contact and identifying what is not ok. This can include shoving or pushing you, physically threatening you, or inappropriate touching in a relationship.
- <u>Emotional boundaries</u>: refers to a person's feelings or emotional health. These boundaries are needed when someone criticizes, insults, or invalidates another person's feelings or trust.

- <u>Material boundaries</u>: refers to money and possessions. This includes setting limits on what you are willing to share, and with whom. Material boundaries address issues such as someone taking or damaging your possessions, or they pressure you into giving or lending them.
- <u>Intellectual boundaries</u>: refers to respecting your thoughts and ideas. These boundaries focus on when someone dismisses, insults, or belittles your thoughts or ideas.
- <u>Sexual boundaries</u>: refers to the emotional, intellectual, and physical aspects of sexuality. These are violated when someone promotes uncomfortable and/or unwanted touching, pressure to engage in sexual acts, or making inappropriate sexual comments. It is important to set boundaries that provide respect and understanding of your personal limits.
- <u>Time boundaries</u>: refers to how a person uses their time or other's time. Time boundaries include situations such as when another person is chronically late, or they demand much of your time. They don't respect that you have other obligations that also require your time.

Once you identify the areas of your relationship that need boundaries, the next step is to learn how to set the boundaries.

Setting Boundaries

There are steps you can take to create and implement boundaries, but you must first believe that you deserve to be treated with respect. It is not ok to be in a situation that abuses you, whether it is physical, emotional, material, intellectual, sexual, or time demanding issues. You are loved and cherished by our Heavenly Father and worthy of being treated with respect.

Once you recognize your right to be respected, take time to identify the boundaries that are needed with your loved one. Write down the areas where you need to set boundaries and include what is acceptable and what is not. Then write down the specific boundary so you can clearly communicate it to your loved one. Be sure to include the consequences that will be enforced if they are not compliant. Make sure your boundaries are doable and that you are willing and able to enforce them.

Once you have identified your boundaries, the next step is to communicate and explain them to your loved one. This needs to be done in a calm and respectful manner, and may need to be repeated until the person understands you are serious. Be prepared for push back. Remain calm and restate your expectations in a loving manner.

One of the boundaries I needed to create for our daughter was in relation to her language. Whenever she was upset, whether it was with us or someone outside the family, her language was extremely foul and abusive. I set a boundary where I would not participate in a conversation when her language was offensive. I would give her one warning and then either hang up the phone or walk away. Once I committed to consistently enforcing this boundary, she knew I was serious. Eventually she was able to stop her inappropriate language, knowing that I would enforce the boundary that was set.

Jesus had to set boundaries while He was doing His ministry here on earth. When He needed time alone with the Father, He set a boundary that allowed Him to separate Himself from the crowds. The Lord recognizes our need for boundaries and below are examples of how Jesus set boundaries:

- Jesus set aside personal prayer time: *"But you, when you pray, go into your room and when you have shut your door, pray to your Father who is in the secret place; and your Father who sees in secret will reward you openly."* Matthew 6:6 NKJV
- Jesus tells us to be honest and direct: *"But let your 'Yes' be 'Yes,' and your 'No,' 'No.' For whatever is more than these is from the evil one."* Matthew 5:37 NKJV
- Jesus instructs us to set priorities: *"No servant can serve two masters; for either he will hate the one and love the other, or else he will be loyal to the one and despise the other. You cannot serve God and mammon."* Luke 16:13 NKJV

Maintaining Boundaries

Maintaining boundaries is a difficult task, especially when there is a lot of push back or manipulation of our emotions. We can create boundaries, but we can't control how our loved one will respond to them. There are some strategies we can implement to help us with enforcing the boundaries when we are struggling or encounter resistance.

One strategy is to flip the focus back to what pushed you to create the boundaries to begin with. Remember why you are setting the boundaries, which is for your well-being and safety. The boundaries you have created are designed to care for your mental, physical, and spiritual health. Focus on the benefits, which are to develop a healthier relationship.

Another strategy is to practice being loving but firm when enforcing the boundaries. Do dress rehearsals practicing your presentation. You should be prepared for when the person crosses the line, and when you need to follow through with the consequences. This can be challenging, especially when it goes against our nature. For example, your loved one may continually ask you for money for gas, social activities, food, etc., and never pay you back even though they say they will. You've established the boundary to not give them money until they have paid you back from the previous loan. They may beg, demand, cry, or try to guilt you into relenting. State your boundary calmly and clearly (repeatedly if necessary), and don't get pulled into an emotional exchange. You may need to have another person there to back you up, and it may involve tabling the conversation until a later time. Creating a written agreement beforehand with your loved one regarding the boundary may be helpful with preventing potential conflicts.

A third strategy is to periodically reevaluate your boundaries and be willing to renegotiate if circumstances have changed. This is not relenting, but making changes as your loved one's behavior has improved or changed. You can always go back to the original boundary if circumstances require you to do so.

Finally, have compassion with yourself. Maintaining boundaries is hard and there may be times when you relinquish or give into their demands. Forgive yourself and reset your mind to stay strong and firm. Ask for support from family and friends. Pray for wisdom and strength when you are tired and weary. Sometimes we need to get away and separate ourselves to refresh our mind and soul.

Scriptures For Maintaining Boundaries:

"He gives power to the weak, and to those who have no might He increases strength." Isaiah 40:29 NKJV

"I will love You, O Lord, my strength. The Lord is my rock and my fortress and my deliverer; My God, my strength, in whom I will trust; My shield and the horn of my salvation, my stronghold." Psalms 18:1-2 NKJV

"But the salvation of the righteous is from the Lord; He is their strength in the time of trouble." Psalms 37:39 NKJV

"In the day when I cried out, You answered me, And made me bold with strength in my soul." Psalms 138:3 NKJV

"But Jesus looked at them and said to them, 'With men this is impossible, but with God all things are possible.'" Matthew 19:26 NKJV

Reflection and Application

1. What type of boundary/boundaries do you identify with and need to implement with your loved one? List the areas below that need to be addressed.

_____

_____

_____

_____

_____

2. Write out your boundaries along with the consequences when they are crossed. Keep it short and simple so it is easy to communicate and enforce.

_____

_____

_____

_____

_____

3. Write out what steps you can take to maintain your boundaries. Who can you ask to help support or encourage you when you are struggling?

_____

_____

_____

_____

_____

Notes and Journaling

Seeking Wisdom and Discernment

Wisdom vs Knowledge

Wisdom and knowledge are both important with all of life's decisions and choices, and it is important to understand the difference. Knowledge is the information we obtain through research, education, and experience. We need to have knowledge about the diseases/illnesses that are impacting either ourselves or our loved ones. Wisdom though, takes it a step further and enables us to apply that knowledge to do what is best and proper. Knowledge is simply knowing the facts; wisdom is having Godly understanding with knowing how to best utilize and apply those facts.

Charles Spurgeon described wisdom in this manner: *Wisdom is the right use of knowledge. To know is not to be wise. Many men know a great deal and are all the greater fools for it. There is no fool so great a fool as a knowing fool. But to know how to use knowledge is to have wisdom.*

Having a loved one with mental illness can place a lot of demands on you and many times you need to make decisions on their behalf. Yes, it is important to have knowledge before making decisions, but even more importantly, we need to have wisdom to help us make the right or best decisions. This leads us to asking how we can obtain and apply that wisdom. True wisdom can only come from God. He wants to bless us with His wisdom, and He gives it freely to those who seek Him and obey His word.

Obtaining Wisdom

As believers in Christ, we have access to God's wisdom. He freely gives us the gift of wisdom, and there are Biblical guidelines that show us how to obtain His wisdom. The first guideline is developing a reverent respect and fear of the Lord. When Jesus taught us to pray in Luke 11 NKJV, the first thing He said in verse 2 was *"...When you pray, say: Our Father in heaven, Hallowed be Your name."* Our heavenly Father is hallowed, holy and sacred. Fearing God means to understand who He truly is, recognizing that He is our sovereign and all-powerful God. Having reverent fear of God inspires us to love and obey Him with our whole heart, mind, soul and strength. Psalm 111:10 NKJV tells us, *"The fear of the Lord is the beginning of wisdom; A good understanding have all those who do His commandments. His praise endures forever."*

Next, we need to have a true desire for His wisdom. We need to seek it, crave it, and hunger for it. Proverbs 2:4-5 NKJV tells us, *"If you seek her as silver, and search for her as for hidden treasures; then you will understand the fear of the Lord, and find the knowledge of God."*

We then need to earnestly pray and ask Him for His wisdom. James 1:5 NKJV says, *"If any of you lacks wisdom, let him ask of God, who gives to all liberally and without reproach, and it will be given to him."* When we ask, He promises to generously supply us with His wisdom.

Finally, to gain a greater understanding of wisdom we must study it in God's word. Psalm 19:7 NKJV tells us, *"The law of the Lord is perfect, converting the soul; The testimony of the Lord is sure, making wise the simple."* There are stories throughout the Bible about people who have been blessed with His wisdom. Read 1 Kings 3:3-15, the story of Solomon being offered anything from God, and he chose to be given wisdom and discernment. Read through Proverbs which Solomon wrote after receiving God's blessing of wisdom and discernment. Allow his story and words of wisdom encourage and motivate you.

Applying Wisdom

Once we have understanding on how to obtain Godly wisdom, the next step is knowing how to apply His wisdom. This requires a commitment to seek and ask for His guidance. It also requires a desire to understand His wisdom and know how to apply it as we are caring for our loved ones.

To apply God's wisdom, we need to first be determined to understand His wisdom. This involves making a commitment to study His word and daily pursue Him. We cannot apply what we do not know or understand. Read Proverbs 2:1-7 where Solomon describes the value of wisdom. He tells us that God gives wisdom to those who incline their ear and apply their heart to understanding. If you ask God for understanding, He will generously give it to you.

Next, we need to be obedient to God's word. He promises that when we are obedient, He will bless us and provide us with His gifts, including His gift of wisdom. Deuteronomy 28: 2 NKJV says, *"And all these blessings shall come upon you and overtake you, because you obey the voice of the Lord your God."* God honors those who are obedient to His word and commands.

We then need to listen and be sensitive to the prompting of the Holy Spirit. The Holy Spirit plays a vital role in our lives by guiding us and instructing us in His wisdom. The Holy Spirit is our Helper as we use His wisdom with making decisions, providing guidance, and communicating with and for our loved ones. Godly wisdom recognizes the crucial role the Holy Spirit plays in our lives.

Finally, we need to seek counsel from people who have spiritual wisdom. We can glean from their experience and knowledge of God's word. Proverbs 13:20 NKJV says, *"He who walks with wise men will be wise, But the companion of fools will be destroyed."* Proverbs 27:17 NKJV also says, *"As iron sharpens iron, So a man sharpens the countenance of his friend."* Having Godly mentors in your life will help you grow in His wisdom and apply it to your daily life. Pastors and church leaders are there to help guide you and pray with you. Get plugged in with a small church group, home fellowship, or ministry where you can be supported and discipled in Godly wisdom. As the church body we are called to support one another and pray for each other.

Discernment

What is discernment and how does it relate to wisdom? Discernment is a spiritual gift that gives us sound judgment and the ability to perceive the difference between right and wrong, good and evil, truth or lies. It helps us to see things clearly when they are not clear or straightforward. It enables us to accurately evaluate information, people, and situations by having a sound understanding of what is true and right. Charles Spurgeon described it as, *Discernment is not knowing the difference between right and wrong, it's knowing the difference between right and almost right.* Wisdom is having spiritual direction as we use and apply knowledge; discernment is the ability to clearly dissect that knowledge and determine if it is based on truth or lies, good or evil.

Wisdom and discernment go hand in hand as we navigate through life and care for our loved ones. When a person is filled with wisdom from the Holy Spirit, they are also walking in discernment. The Holy Spirit gives us discernment so that we can clearly recognize and distinguish between what is coming from God, Satan, or the influence of the world.

As my journey with raising a mentally ill daughter grew more challenging, I became more and more dependent on God for His wisdom and discernment. I needed His wisdom as I made decisions with choosing the right doctor and psychiatrist, finding the right therapist, and managing her medication and treatment plan. I needed His wisdom when communicating with her teachers about her challenges, and meeting yearly with them to review her accommodations in the classroom. I needed His discernment when her behaviors worsened and I had to determine which of her behaviors were due to her illness, and which were from her own rebellion and choice. I needed His discernment when I encountered professionals and people who shared their advice or opinions. I needed His discernment to decipher what was truth and what were lies. I often struggled with whether I was receiving a message from the Lord or being attacked by the enemy, Satan, the father of lies. It was through His wisdom and discernment that I was able to navigate through some very rough waters. It was His wisdom and discernment that gave me clarity, peace, and courage.

Scriptures For Wisdom and Discernment:

"Trust in the Lord with all your heart, And lean not on your own understanding; In all your ways acknowledge Him, And He shall direct your paths." Proverbs 3:5-6 NKJV

"If any of you lacks wisdom, let him ask of God, who gives to all liberally and without reproach, and it will be given to him." James 1:5 NKJV

"Therefore whoever hears these sayings of Mine, and does them, I will liken him to a wise man who built his house on the rock: and the rain descended, the floods came, and the winds blew and beat on that house; and it did not fall, for it was founded on the rock." Matthew 7:24-25 NKJV

"Oh, the depth of the riches both of the wisdom and knowledge of God! How unsearchable are His judgments and His ways past finding out!" Romans 11:33 NKJV

Reflection and Application

1. In your own words, what is your understanding of wisdom? How do we obtain and apply wisdom in our lives?

_____

_____

_____

_____

2. Describe in your own words your definition of Discernment. How are wisdom and discernment similar? How are they different? How do they work together?

_____

_____

_____

_____

3. How can you apply wisdom and discernment in your own life and/or your loved one's life? Be specific about areas where you need wisdom and discernment.

_____

_____

_____

_____

4. Did any of the included or listed Bible verses speak to you? Write out one or more of the scriptures and meditate on them this week.

_____

_____

_____

_____

Notes and Journaling

CHAPTER 9

Silencing Shame

Feelings Experienced with a Mental Illness Diagnosis

When a loved one is diagnosed with a mental illness, we need to recognize that their illness is often due to a biological component. They have a disease attacking their brain. It is not a result of bad parenting or lack of support, and there isn't anything you could have done or done differently to change their diagnosis. Even with recognizing this, we still experience a range of powerful emotions.

One of the common emotions we may experience is feeling ashamed, hurt, or embarrassed over our loved one's behaviors. We cannot control them, and at times they can even escalate as we try to redirect or stop their behaviors. Family gatherings, especially over the holidays, can be impacted or even ruined by our loved one's actions. Feelings of anger, frustration, and embarrassment are often a result.

Having a loved one with mental illness often leaves us dealing with their fall out. Their stressful behaviors can occur in public or in front of friends and family. We are often left with feelings of despair from the shame we experience, and unless others have experienced it themselves, they often don't understand the day-to-day struggles of dealing with a loved one with mental illness. We see their looks of blame, exasperation, and see they are uncomfortable. Sometimes they avoid us and make excuses so they can bow out of family gatherings. Sometimes we are even accused of being the cause of our loved one's emotional or behavioral problems. This can make us want to withdraw and compounds our feelings of shame.

Another consequence of feeling shame and embarrassment is when we, ourselves, withdraw from our loved one. We are exhausted from dealing with the range of emotions caused by their behaviors. We are tired of being publicly embarrassed and dealing with the unpredictability of their actions. We never know what is going to set them off and feel like we are walking on eggshells. We are weary, emotionally drained, and at a loss with knowing how to deal with our loved one. We feel shame over our need to withdraw from them because of the constant stress and embarrassment.

When we are feeling shame and embarrassment over our loved one's illness, we may choose to try and hide our issues. We want to protect ourselves and our immediate family members from further embarrassment and humiliation. We want to give the impression that all is well to the outside world. In reality, our friends and family are often aware of our situation and may not know what to say or do to help us. They may feel uncomfortable, so nobody discusses the problem which further isolates us from the support we need. It becomes the elephant in the room that no one wants to talk about.

Managing Shame with Family and Friends

When your loved one's behaviors are difficult to manage, one of the first things you should do is contact a professional (physician, therapist, and/or organization) for guidance. If your loved one is an adult, you will be limited with being able to discuss your concerns with their healthcare provider. They are protected by HIPPA, and a release will need to be signed by your loved one giving you permission to speak with them. This is often an obstacle where professional organizations such as NAMI (National Alliance on Mental Illness) can provide support. NAMI is nationwide and you can access your local organization on their website (NAMI.org). They have counselors and volunteers who have experience and are available as a resource. They understand your shame and embarrassment first-hand.

It is also important to reach out for support by initiating a conversation with your close family and friends. Be open about your loved one's diagnosis and the mental health challenges they are experiencing. Share with them your own feelings about your loved one's illness and let them know your concerns. Being honest about what you are going through can help ease the shame. If they have difficulty understanding, then give them resources that explain your loved one's illness. Sometimes comparing mental illness with a physical illness can bring clarity. For example, if someone has Asthma it is not due to their choice or doing. They need medication and treatment to manage their symptoms and restore efficient breathing. It is a medical disease and not their fault. Mental illness is no different. Our loved one did not choose to be mentally ill. They have a medical disease of the brain that requires treatment to restore proper function. Be prepared for the possibility that your conversations with family and friends may be awkward or uncomfortable, but being honest and getting things out in the open can bring understanding to your loved one's behaviors. Not everyone is going to be receptive, and they may feel uncomfortable or even experience fear. Mental illness still has a stigma in society, and unfortunately there are many violent incidents reported on the news involving mentally ill individuals. Many families have been left shattered by their loved one's actions.

It is so important to realize and understand that your loved one's illness and behaviors are NOT a result of, or a reflection on your parenting or care taking. You can do everything right and provide the best care, but you still cannot control your loved one's behaviors or actions. Especially as adults, they need to be willing to get treatment and follow the treatment plan. They also need to be willing to work with their doctors and therapists to achieve stability. You cannot force them (unless they say they are going to harm themselves or others) to get treatment. Their choices do not and should not place shame on you. This is where God's healing around shame can restore us and give us hope.

God's Healing in Shame

Having a mentally ill loved one can cause us to experience shame for things that are outside of our control. We often feel frustrated and overwhelmed, and the embarrassment can keep us from seeking the support we need from family, friends, and agencies. Understanding shame from God's perspective can set us free as we study His word and promises.

Shame and guilt have been present since the creation of Adam and Eve. They experienced shame when they were disobedient to God and ate the forbidden fruit. They felt shame when they became aware of their nakedness and tried to hide from God. Despite their sin and shame, God had compassion and made them clothing out of skins and covered their nakedness. He removed their shame.

God continues to remove our shame today, whether it is due to our own sin or the sin of our loved one. When we feel shame and guilt, we need to remember and believe that the blood Jesus shed on the cross has covered us and set us free from our sin and shame. Even when our loved one is responsible for bringing us shame, God's word urges us to let go of it and glorify Him instead. 1 Peter 4:16 NKJV tells us, *"Yet if anyone suffers as a Christian, let him not be ashamed, but let him glorify God in this matter."*

As believers in Christ, we know that Jesus bore our shame. He is our example of ultimate suffering and shame as He endured His trial, crucifixion, and death. He was deserted by His disciples, mocked, beaten, whipped, and spat on. Yet He bore it all, knowing it was for God's divine purpose. Even though He asked God to take away His cup (Matthew 26: 39, 42), He recognized and submitted to God's will. He surrendered everything, including His shame, to His Father knowing that He would be glorified.

Our loved one's behaviors may not change, but when we surrender our shame, we allow God to bring glory out of our pain and hardship. We allow His healing to take place in our lives, which enables the Holy Spirit to work within us and our loved one. We can claim Romans 8:1

NKJV, *"There is therefore now no condemnation to those who are in Christ Jesus, who do not walk according to the flesh, but according to the Spirit."* When we walk in the Spirit and claim His truth and promises, we are walking in His light and hope. We are set free from guilt and shame. There is no shame or condemnation in Christ Jesus!

Scripture Verses to Claim over Shame

"They cried to You, and were delivered; They trusted in You, and were not ashamed." Psalms 22:5 NKJV

"In You, O Lord, I put my trust; Let me never be ashamed; Deliver me in Your righteousness." Psalms 31:1 NKJV

"There is therefore now no condemnation to those who are in Christ Jesus, who do not walk according to the flesh, but according to the Spirit." Romans 8:1 NKJV

"Be diligent to present yourself approved to God, a worker who does not need to be ashamed, rightly dividing the word of truth." II Timothy 2:15 NKJV

Reflection and Application

1. Are you experiencing feelings of embarrassment or shame with your loved one? Have they kept you from seeking support?

_____

_____

_____

_____

2. Has shame over your loved one's behaviors impacted your relationships with family members or friends? If so, how have they been impacted?

_____

_____

_____

_____

3. Have you been able to have a conversation with your family/friends regarding your loved one's mental illness? If yes, what was their response? If not, do you feel comfortable having this conversation?

_____

_____

_____

_____

4. How does God's word encourage you with overcoming shame? What scripture can you claim this week if you struggle with feelings of shame?

_____

_____

_____

_____

Notes and Journaling

CHAPTER 10

Protecting Your Family and Marriage

Impact on Family Dynamics

When mental illness is initially diagnosed with a loved one, a common response is denial. Family members may deny that the illness is more than just an acute episode or a one-time crisis. When the initial crisis is over, everyone feels relief and they are ready for life to go back to normal. They want to put the episode behind them and focus on the future. It is easy to believe that now that the symptoms are better, they are fine and the worse is behind them. Remaining in a state of denial though, can prevent the family from accepting their loved one's illness. It can delay them with recognizing their loved one's warning signs, and consequently end up in another crisis situation. In addition to denial, some family members may be able to grasp the reality of the illness while others cannot. Those who accept the diagnosis may end up taking on the role of being the protector for the mentally ill loved one. This can create tension and conflict within the family and damage relationships.

In addition, family members may have little information or understanding of their loved one's mental illness. They may feel the illness is due to the loved one's choice or believe that there is no hope for a positive future for them. The illness may seem to control the outlook and future for the family, and there can be feelings of depression and despair. It is important for families to seek resources and gather information to help them understand how the illness affects their loved one. They need to understand how medication and/or therapy treatment can help them achieve long term stability. But this can also create conflict within the family. Some family members may be against medication or believe therapy is a waste of time and money. There may also be financial stressors that are an issue.

The family may also feel reluctant to share or discuss their loved one's illness with others, not knowing how they will react. Many people have very strong opinions about mental illness, which is typically attributed to a lack of knowledge. They may be fearful and uncomfortable discussing your loved one's diagnosis. There is a lot of misinformation out there, and mental illness is often blamed for violent occurrences. Family members may also be reluctant to invite people over to their home because of the unpredictability of their loved one's behavior. They never know what is going to set them off or what they might say or do. The loved one may also be so ill that the family is afraid to leave them home alone. As a result, they either don't go out, or go out separately to be sure that someone is always there to keep their loved one safe. These factors can lead the family to becoming isolated.

In addition, people may have difficulty understanding the reality of mental illness. Families often feel they have no other choice but to withdraw from previous relationships to protect their loved one and themselves. This can cause some families to even withdraw from their church and fellowship. They believe that the church may blame them or not understand. This is where it is so important for the church body to gain knowledge and have a better understanding of mental illness.

Common Issues within the Family

Family members commonly experience frustration when living with a mentally ill loved one. They can feel frustrated when their loved one seems to ignore their responsibilities or lack motivation to get better. The family may feel like they are deliberately trying to make their lives harder. They may also feel frustrated when it seems like their loved one is not improving. It often takes several weeks for medication to be effective, especially with depression, and that waiting period can be difficult. It is hard to understand why they won't just "snap out of it" and be normal again. Families may also feel frustrated when they cannot return to their normal way of life that they previously took for granted. They miss the person their loved one used to be and miss the life they had together. If they stay focused on the past instead of on the current reality, it can lead to more frustration and conflict.

The constant stress of having a loved one with mental illness can lead to serious family issues. Life within the home has become unpredictable and unsettled. What used to be normal, such as vacations or family gatherings, have become very challenging or nonexistent. The needs of the mentally ill loved one has taken precedence over the needs of the family. This is especially hard on siblings. They may feel like their needs are being put aside or don't take priority. The entire focus and energy within the family has been placed solely on the one who is mentally ill. This can also take a toll on the marriage. Parents may disagree on how to manage their child's treatment or behavior within the home. They may also be too exhausted to give attention to each other. If the illness involves an extended family member or adult sibling, they may feel they need to protect their own immediate family, which can create conflict within the extended family. These factors can drain the family and damage relationships. There may be long term painful feelings that go unresolved.

Exhaustion and Burnout within the Family

It is understandable that families can become worn out and discouraged when caring for a loved one who is mentally ill. They may feel discouraged because everything they have tried has not helped or improved the situation with their loved one. Or they may be burned out trying to help a loved one who does not want help. They may feel trapped and exhausted, especially if they don't have the needed support from other family members. They may feel they have no control over their lives and are unable to predict the future.

Burnout within the family can be a result of the ill loved one having no limits set on their behavior. This may be due to the family feeling fearful or having a prior experience of a severe response. The result is that the loved one ends up consuming all their energy. They may be threatening, demanding, or refusing to alter their behavior. They may not even see or understand the effect their behavior is having on the family. Their focus is on themselves. As a result, families often decide that they can no longer live with the abusive behavior, threats, or fear. The family may be forced to make the difficult decision to either remove their loved one from the home, or possibly place them in a residential treatment facility. Even this decision can cause trauma and conflict within the family.

Grief Within the Family

One of the most difficult things for families to accept, is the reality of the life altering impact their loved one's illness may have on them. Their hopes and dreams for their loved one's future have changed, and they may struggle with letting go of prior expectations. This is especially true if the illness has impaired their loved one's ability to function and participate in normal activities of daily life. It is difficult as the family watches others finish their education, obtain jobs, and begin to live independent lives. Meanwhile they are watching their own loved one struggle, unable to support themselves or live on their own. They sometimes cannot maintain friendships due to their illness and become more and more isolated.

Grief within the family is often focused on the loss of what might have been for their loved one. They struggle with being able to see the possibilities that remain for them. Resetting expectations can enable the family to help their loved one find their strengths and talents. They can create a "new normal" and explore with them possible jobs or careers. The entire family can be involved and have input.

Our daughter struggled with mental illness, and we had to reset our expectations for her education and future. Her initial goal in school was to become an elementary school teacher. She loved children and had a true gift working with them. She was able to connect with kids and they responded to her. When her illness worsened and she repeatedly dropped her community college classes due to anxiety and stress, we had to accept that she would not be able to complete the schooling required to become a teacher. We then explored other options that would allow her to work with children and did not require a college degree. She was able to get a job with the school district working in a classroom with special needs children. She loved her job, and it boosted her confidence as she was successful working with these children.

God's Healing

Families may have difficulty moving beyond the impact that mental illness has had on them. They see other families having "normal" lives and focus on all they have lost. They may ask God "why is this happening?" There is no clear answer except we live in a fallen world that is filled with sin and sickness. Mental illness is a disease that can strike anyone like cancer, heart disease, or diabetes. God does not want us to live in a state of despair or hopelessness. Instead, He offers us hope and strength as we walk this difficult path, and provides guidelines to help us on this journey.

The first guideline is for us to remain calm and seek His peace. Our tendency is to panic and worry. God has promised to give us strength when we are weak, and peace when we are feeling anxious. Read Philippians 4: 6-7. He tells us to remain calm, so we can think clearly and make the right decisions for our loved one and family. He wants us to trust Him and believe that He is keeping our family in His loving hands.

The next guideline is for us to recognize the importance of being wise. In addition to having knowledge and understanding about your loved one's illness, it is necessary to have wisdom so that you can make sound decisions about your loved one's care. Wisdom is important with choosing the right doctor or therapist, communicating with health care providers, advocating for your loved one(s), or making decisions for the needs of your family. Turn to God and seek His wisdom so He can guide you on the best steps to take.

The Lord also reminds us of the importance of obedience. As you care for your loved one, you will be influenced by friends and family members as they share their advice and opinions. But the advice they give may not be based on Biblical guidelines. It is important to go to His word when you need sound counsel and to listen to the leading of the Holy Spirit. There will be times when you need to make difficult, heart-wrenching decisions for your mentally ill loved one. It is vital that you remain obedient to Gods' Word, so He can guide you in making sound decisions.

God's word also gives us the guideline that we need to practice patience. With most illnesses, there are treatments that provide fast results and/or a complete recovery. With mental illness though, response to medication can take weeks, months, or even longer before there is any improvement. Even then the dosage may need adjusting, or the medication changed due to not having the desired effect. This is very trying for the family and the impacted loved one and can lead to frustration or despair. You may become angry at God for not answering your prayers, and feel He is distant. It is important in these times, that you make it a priority to spend time alone with God. Spend time in prayer and search the scriptures for passages that bring hope and comfort. Allow the Holy Spirit to guide you as you learn how to wait, trust, and rest in His promises. Remember that He uses these times to strengthen your faith and relationship with Jesus Christ.

Finally, the Lord encourages us to be ready for action. After the initial trauma of the mental illness diagnosis, there will be a time for action and decision making. Seek Him for guidance on the next steps to take. It is not only important to seek care for your loved one, but also for yourself and other family members. Remember that the Lord will be faithful to lead you in the right direction, but you need to be willing to step out in faith and trust Him.

Scripture for Healing Within the Family

"Behold, I will bring it health and healing; I will heal them and reveal to them the abundance of peace and truth." Jeremiah 33:6 NKJV

"Bless the Lord, O my soul, and forget not all His benefits: Who forgives all your iniquities, who heals all your diseases, Who redeems your life from destruction, Who crowns you with loving kindness and tender mercies." Psalms 103:2-4 NKJV

"Then your light shall break forth like the morning, your healing shall spring forth speedily, and your righteousness shall go before you; the glory of the Lord shall be your rear guard." Isaiah 58:8 NKJV

Reflection and Application

1. How has your loved one's illness and diagnosis impacted your family? Are there issues causing pain and conflict within your family?

_____

_____

_____

_____

2. Do you often feel frustration with your loved one? In what ways? How do you manage your frustration?

_____

_____

_____

_____

3. Have you or are you experiencing burnout? What steps can you take to help reduce your feelings of exhaustion and burnout? How can you take care of yourself?

_____

_____

_____

_____

4. Which of God's guidelines can you apply to your life as you are dealing with your loved one? What steps can you take to implement them?

_____

_____

_____

_____

Notes and Journaling

CHAPTER 11

Importance of Self-Care

Tips to Manage Stressors

Being a caregiver can be extremely stressful and oftentimes affects our health. Common symptoms of stress include having headaches, low energy, gastrointestinal issues, tension causing aches and pains, as well as insomnia. This continued stress can take a toll on you and on your relationships. To help you manage your stress levels, it is important that you first identify what your stressors are and how they make you feel. Certain situations or circumstances may make you feel frustrated, angry, or overwhelmed. Identifying which ones are causing you stress can help you decide how to manage them.

To manage or alleviate your stress load, you need to be willing to eliminate or modify some situations. For example, you may find that when you go shopping with your loved one, they often demand that you buy them items and will argue with you if you refuse. To alleviate this stressor, you will need to set agreed upon boundaries beforehand, and let them know there will be consequences. If they choose to not abide by the pre-set boundaries, then inform them they will not be allowed to go with you next time. If you stick with your boundary, eventually they will understand that you are serious about changing their behavior and eliminating this stressor.

As caregivers we can sometimes feel overwhelmed. Your loved one may have multiple needs or issues that require your input, support, and time. When you reflect on the numerous needs and demands placed on you at that moment, you can feel overwhelmed or discouraged. To manage these feelings, it helps to focus on one issue or problem at a time. For example, instead of looking at an entire puzzle with multiple pieces, try to break it down and focus on one piece at a time. As you are successful with managing one piece, then move onto the next. Try not to focus on the enormity of the whole problem or issue. Break it down into small pieces and baby steps. You may need to ask for help or support if you are feeling overwhelmed. Allow others to come along beside you and help ease your burdens.

We all have our personal limits. It's okay to take a step back and focus on yourself, so you can recharge your battery to keep going. If your physical and/or mental health are being negatively impacted, then you are not in a good position to provide care for your loved one. You may need to communicate to your family and loved one that you need a break or vacation from all the stress and demands. If necessary, seek support from professional resources. This may include getting counseling for yourself or getting involved with a support group. Spend time nurturing yourself and replenishing your personal reserves.

Taking Care of Your Health

Living with a mentally ill loved one is not easy. It can be exhausting. As caregivers it is important to not lose sight of your own needs and health. Recognize that to effectively take care of your loved one, you need to take care of yourself. Think about when you are on an airplane. As part of the safety measures, you are instructed by the flight crew to put on your own oxygen mask first before you try to help others. When you take care of your needs and health first, then you are in a better place to take care of the needs of others.

Part of making your health a priority is taking time to schedule your routine exams with your primary healthcare provider. Be prepared to discuss and be honest about your situation and the amount of stress you are currently enduring. Your healthcare provider may be able to provide you with information, resources and referrals to help support you.

It is also important to practice a healthy lifestyle, so you are feeling your best physically and mentally. Below are some basic strategies you can apply to help maintain and/or improve your health:

- Be aware of your eating habits. Over or under eating is common when under high levels of stress. Make sure your diet includes fruits and vegetables, lean protein, and whole grains. Limit high sugar and high fat foods. You can ask your healthcare provider for a referral to a dietician to review your current diet and provide information to improve your nutrition.
- Try to get 8 hours of sleep a night. Difficulty sleeping or insomnia is also common when stressed. Some things you can do to improve your sleep include:

  - Avoid caffeinated drinks in the afternoon or evening.

- ▪ Turn off or stop engaging with electronic devices (TV, cell phones, tablets, computers) at least 30 minutes before going to bed.
- ▪ There are natural products you can use that help with sleep. Be sure to discuss your sleep issues with your healthcare provider for guidance and recommendations.

- Try to get some form of daily exercise or activity. The CDC recommends that adults get at least 150 minutes of moderate intensity exercise each week. You can choose to exercise for 30 minutes a day five days a week, or exercise for 50 minutes a day three days a week. This can include walking, swimming, pickleball, or whatever you find enjoyable and can fit into your schedule.
- Find activities that help you relax. This can include spending time in prayer, reading, breathing exercises, doing crafts or artwork, playing or listening to music, whatever helps you to relax.
- Minimize consuming products that have high levels of caffeine or stimulants. This includes coffee, caffeinated tea, sodas, energy drinks, and chocolate. Stimulants can cause feelings of anxiety or nervousness and interfere with sleep.
- Limit or eliminate consuming alcohol, drugs and tobacco.

Burnout

As caregivers we are at risk of experiencing burnout. This can happen when we become so busy helping our loved ones that we neglect our own physical, emotional, and spiritual health. The demands we place on ourselves can eventually lead us to feeling hopeless, overwhelmed, exhausted, and eventual burnout. Common factors that can lead to burnout include:

- Unable to separate roles: sometimes family members become consumed when thrust into the role of a caregiver. It can be difficult for them to separate their role as a caregiver from their role as a spouse, sibling, child, or other close relationship.
- Unrealistic expectations: the caregiver may expect their involvement will fix or cure their loved one's illness. This can lead to feelings of disappointment, frustration, and even failure.
- Inability to control factors: Caregivers can become frustrated by financial burdens and/or lack of resources. They may not have the skills to effectively plan, manage and organize their loved one's care.
- Unreasonable demands: Caregivers themselves, or other family members may place unreasonable burdens upon them. Managing their loved one's care becomes their exclusive responsibility.
- Loss of Insight: Caregivers may not recognize that they are suffering burnout and may be unable to function effectively. They may even become ill themselves.

The ability to recognize symptoms of burnout is important for the caregiver and family. Symptoms of burnout are similar to symptoms of depression:

Withdrawal (from friends and family)
Lost interest in activities previously enjoyed
Feeling depressed, anxious, hopeless or helpless
Changes in appetite, weight or both
Changes in sleep patterns (difficulty sleeping or excessive sleep)
More frequent illnesses
Feeling you want to hurt yourself or the person you are caring for
Experiencing emotional and/or physical exhaustion
Irritability

Burnout Prevention

If you or a family member are showing signs of burnout, there are practical strategies you can use to prevent burnout from occurring or worsening:

- Confide in someone you trust. Share with them your situation and the feelings you are experiencing.
- Set realistic goals for yourself. Recognize that you need help with the caregiving, and if possible, delegate responsibilities to other family members. You may need to contact an outside agency for support.
- Educate yourself about your loved one's diagnosis. Understand the long-term outlook and treatment they may require.
- Don't neglect yourself because you are too busy caring for others. Taking care of yourself is a necessity, not a luxury.
- Talk to a professional if you are feeling overwhelmed or depressed. This can include a therapist, social worker, or pastor at your church.
- Recognize your limits and look at your situation honestly. If you are starting to see signs of burnout, reach out for support from someone.
- Develop healthy ways of coping. This can include exercising, listening to music, spending time with friends, or getting into a support group. Figure out what helps you to feel calmer and reduces your stress.

God's Perspective and Word on Self-Care

When God created the world, He Himself set aside the seventh day as a holy day to rest from all work. He spoke to us in Genesis 2:3 NIV: *"Then God blessed the seventh day and made it holy, because on it He rested from all the work of creating that He had done."* God didn't rest because He needed it, He did it to model the importance of rest for us. He knows we need to rest to replenish ourselves so we can keep serving Him well. With our fast-paced lifestyle, we tend to feel guilty when we take time to relax and rest. If you struggle with this remind yourself of the example God has set for us.

God has also taught us to not just rest, but to put aside a day of sabbath rest. He instructed us in Leviticus 23:3 NIV, *"There are six days when you may work, but the seventh day is a day of sabbath rest, a day of sacred assembly. You are not to do any work; wherever you live, it is a sabbath to the Lord."* He knows we need to restore ourselves by spending time in worship, study, and fellowship. When we take time each weekend to invest in our walk with the Lord, we will feel a deeper connection with Him that will carry us through the rest of the week. We need spiritual replenishment to continue caring for our loved one, and as we do, we are serving Him.

The Lord also wants us to come to Him and rest in His presence when we are exhausted and at the end of our rope. He comforts us in Psalm 23: 1-2 NIV, *"The Lord is my shepherd, I lack nothing. He makes me lie down in green pastures, he leads me beside quiet waters, he refreshes my soul."* He is our Shepherd who leads us beside peaceful streams and lets us rest in the green pastures of His abundance. He promises to provide all we need as we care for our loved one.

The Lord knows that we will have times when we just need to cry out to Him. He wants us to come before Him when we are at our limits. He will provide the peace and comfort we need in those times of exhaustion and despair. He tells us in Psalm 34: 17-18 NKJV, *"The righteous cry out, and the Lord hears, and delivers them out of all their troubles. The Lord is near to those who have a broken heart, and saves such as have a contrite heart."* He wants us to come to Him and cry out "Abba, Father." He has big shoulders and wants your honest feelings. He will never stop loving you. Remember that nothing can separate us from the love of God (Romans 8: 38-39).

Reflection and Application

1. What are some stressors that you are experiencing now? Are you willing/able to modify or eliminate some of the demands that are causing you stress? How will you do this?

_____

_____

_____

_____

2. What steps are you taking to improve or maintain your health? Are there any strategies that you are willing to implement or commit to?

_____

_____

_____

_____

3. Have you or are you experiencing symptoms of burnout? Which of the prevention steps can you implement to help reduce your risk of burnout?

_____

_____

_____

_____

4. Were you encouraged with God's command about rest? How can you apply His instructions for rest?

_____

_____

_____

_____

Notes and Journaling

CHAPTER 12

Developing Resilience

What is Resilience?

The American Psychological Association describes resilience as the process and outcome of successfully adapting to difficult or challenging life experiences. It is the ability to adapt well while facing adversity, trauma, threats, tragedy, or severe stress. It is being able to work through emotional pain and allowing yourself to move forward and grow.

Being resilient is not something that you are born with or that occurs automatically. It requires developing a skill set that is worked on and grows over time. It takes time, strength, and support from friends and family. A person's ability to be resilient can depend on a variety of factors, including their own personal skills (e.g. coping skills) and their own personal support system (resources and family/friends).

Resilience is an important skill because it allows a person to process and overcome hardship. Without resilience, you are at risk of being easily overwhelmed and may turn to unhealthy coping behaviors. Developing resilience allows you to tap into your own strengths and support networks, and will enable you to overcome challenges.

Becoming Resilient

Resiliency is something that takes time and experience to develop. Unfortunately, it is through pain and hardships that we learn ways to survive and overcome. Some individuals have difficulty developing healthy skills that enable them to endure trials and hardships. If you struggle with being able to move on or overcome hardships, below is a list of strategies you can apply to help build and strengthen your resiliency.

1. Build a support network of connections and relationships. Connecting with supportive people can provide comfort and remind you that you are not alone in your difficulties. Focus on finding trustworthy friends and family who will listen and encourage you. Traumatic events can cause some individuals to become isolated, but it is important to allow people to help you and support you. Even if you feel like you need to be alone, make sure to schedule time with friends and family.

2. Join a group that will provide support and help you to reclaim hope. The church body wants to support and encourage you, and it is important to surround yourself with caring individuals. Look for support groups that deal with the same issues you are currently facing and can help you through difficult situations.

3. Support overall wellness and take care of your body. Stress impacts your physical body as well as your mind and emotions. Make sure to promote a healthy lifestyle that includes good nutrition, ample sleep (8-9 hours), and regular exercise. Taking care of yourself will help you to better adapt to stress.

4. Calm your mind through prayer, meditating on scripture, listening to music, and/or journaling. Focus on the positive aspects of your life and the blessings you have been given. Make a list of the things you are grateful for and work on seeing your glass half full.

5. Find purpose by serving or helping others. When you help others in need you can gain a sense of purpose which allows you to shift the focus off your problems. Volunteering helps to foster self-worth, and as you help others it can empower you to become more resilient.

6. Refocus or change your perspective when you are faced with problems. Instead of focusing on the impact of the problem, find ways to manage it. You may need to break it down into manageable parts and deal with one part at a time. It is okay to ask for help with managing the problem.

7. Develop realistic goals and formulate a plan that will allow you to accomplish those goals. Focus on one small part of a goal each day that you can achieve, and as you are successful it will build a sense of accomplishment. For example, it can be an exercise plan where you start with 15 minutes and work towards achieving a 60-minute exercise routine.

8. Look back on how you have managed previous hardships. See where you have grown and become more resilient with each situation. Look at the positives that have come out of previous situations, such as having better family relationships or a greater sense of strength. It may help to keep a journal when you are going through trials so you can look back at answered prayers and the ways you were able to endure.

9. Refocus your mind on healthy thoughts. Try to keep things in perspective and recognize when your mind is going down a dark path. Refocus on the positive. Even though you may not be able to change a situation, you can change how you respond or interpret it.

10. Accept change and recognize that it is a part of life. Accepting that you can't stop things from changing, will help you in figuring out how you can embrace the change and manage it.

11. Maintain hope. Focus on the eternal hope we have in our Heavenly Father, and don't allow worry or fear to take hold and consume you. Live with the expectation that God will bring blessings out of your hardships.

12. Learn from past trials. Looking back at how you handled previous hardships can help you examine what worked and what didn't. Recall who and what helped you to get through a difficult situation. Remind yourself of how you were able to gain the strength to move forward. Learn from those experiences.

13. Seek help when you need it. Don't allow shame or embarrassment to keep you from reaching out to friends and family. Sometimes we may need professional help with coping, and that is okay. It takes strength to recognize and obtain professional support when we need it.

Faith Based Resilience

Resiliency in the Bible is often referred to as perseverance, which is a common theme in scripture. It is also referred to as patience, endurance, and long suffering, which are character qualities that God develops in us through trials and hardships. Jesus is our ultimate model for perseverance, which is described in Hebrews 12:1-3 NKJV, *"Therefore we also, since we are surrounded by so great a cloud of witnesses, let us lay aside every weight, and the sin which so easily ensnares us, and let us run with endurance the race that is set before us, looking unto Jesus, the author and finisher of our faith, who for the joy that was set before Him endured the cross, despising the shame, and has sat down at the right hand of the throne of God. For consider Him who endured such hostility from sinners against Himself, lest you become weary and discouraged in your souls."* Jesus persevered through rejection, abuse, being despised, and ultimately death on the cross. He did this by looking to His Father and spending time in prayer as He continued His ministry here on earth. He is our perfect example and our partner as we run our race. He is not only waiting at the finish line but is running right beside us. He picks us up when we trip or fall and guides us until we reach our heavenly home. He is our source of resilience as we persevere in our race.

Paul is another example of resilience in the New Testament. He testified that God's strength was made perfect in his weakness in 2 Corinthians 12: 9-11, *"And He said to me, 'My grace is sufficient for you, for My strength is made perfect in weakness.' Therefore most gladly I will rather boast in my infirmities, that the power of Christ may rest upon me. Therefore I take pleasure in infirmities, in reproaches, in needs, in persecutions, in distresses, for Christ's sake. For when I am weak, then I am strong."* Paul shows us that God does not leave us on our own to develop resiliency. We have the power of Christ within us to endure hardships. As we walk with Him and put our trust in His faithfulness, He will provide the strength that we need.

As we look at examples of people in the Bible, we discover that resiliency comes from God Himself as He nudges and guides us to move forward. Even when situations seem overwhelming, He wants us to trust Him and keep going. We may stumble and fall, but it is important to remember to forgive ourselves and refocus our trust on Him. When we stand firm and persevere in trying times, we honor God's will.

Finally, and most importantly, it is faith that makes us resilient. Through faith we can endure difficult trials and circumstances because we know we are not alone. Faith helps us to find meaning in our hardships knowing that God causes everything to work together for the good. He turns our ashes into beauty. He will bring joy in the morning, even in our darkest nights.

Scripture Verses For Resilience:

"My brethren, count it all joy when you fall into various trials, knowing that the testing of your faith produces patience. But let patience have its perfect work, that you may be perfect and complete, lacking nothing." James 1:2-4 NKJV

"In this you greatly rejoice, though now for a little while, if need be, you have been grieved by various trials, that the genuineness of your faith, being much more precious than gold that perishes, though it is tested by fire, may be found to praise, honor, and glory at the revelation of Jesus Christ." I Peter 1:6-7 NKJV

"And not only that, but we also glory in tribulations, knowing that tribulation produces perseverance; and perseverance, character; and character, hope. Now hope does not disappoint, because the love of God has been poured out in our hearts by the Holy Spirit who was given to us." Romans 5:3-5 NKJV

"And the light shines in the darkness, and the darkness did not comprehend it." John 1:5 NKJV

Reflection and Application

1. Do you feel you have developed resiliency? Which areas do you feel you are resilient? Which situations or areas do you feel you need to improve your resiliency?

_____

_____

_____

_____

2. What steps or strategies can you take to help strengthen your resiliency? You can refer to the ones listed or create your own.

_____

_____

_____

_____

3. In what ways can you allow the Lord to help you with perseverance or resiliency? Did any of the listed verses speak to you? If not, search for other scriptures that speak about perseverance and trials. Write out the verse(s) below to meditate and reflect on.

_____

_____

_____

_____

Notes and Journaling

CHAPTER 13

Holding Fast to Our Hope

What is Hope?

"Hope" is a word or belief that can be viewed from different perspectives. The world's view of hope is often seen as wishful thinking. It has no certainty for a good outcome, and it is not a source of comfort. It is basically keeping your fingers crossed hoping that things will turn out for the good. It is saying "I'm not sure if this is going to happen, but I am hoping it does."

As Christians, believers in Christ, our hope comes with absolute certainty. God always keeps His promises, and we have the certainty that what He has promised will come to pass. Deuteronomy 7:9 NKJV tells us, *"Therefore know that the Lord your God, He is God, the faithful God who keeps covenant and mercy for a thousand generations with those who love Him and keep His commandments."* God's promises are recorded throughout the Bible, and these promises are the foundation of our hope. Below are some of the promises that He has given us:

1. <u>He Gives Us Strength:</u> *"My flesh and my heart fail; But God is the strength of my heart and my portion forever."* Psalms 73:26 NKJV
2. <u>He Promises Rest:</u> *"Come to Me, all you who labor and are heavy laden, and I will give you rest."* Matthew 11:28 NKJV

3. <u>He Takes Care of All Our Needs:</u> *"And my God shall supply all your needs according to His riches in glory by Christ Jesus."* Philippians 4:19 NKJV

4. <u>He Answers Our Prayers:</u> *"For everyone who asks receives, and he who seeks finds, and to him who knocks it will be opened."* Matthew 7:8 NKJV

5. <u>He Works All Things for The Good:</u> *"And we know that all things work together for good to those who love God, to those who are called according to His purpose."* Romans 8:28 NKJV

6. <u>He Is Always with Us:</u> *"Never the less I am continually with You; You hold me by my right hand. You will guide me with Your counsel, And afterward receive me to glory."* Psalms 73:23-24 NKJV

7. <u>He Promises Us Protection:</u> *"Though I walk in the midst of trouble, You will revive me; You will stretch out Your hand Against the wrath of my enemies, And Your right hand will save me."* Psalms 138:7 NKJV

8. <u>He Forgives Our Sins:</u> *"In Him we have redemption through His blood, the forgiveness of sins, according to the riches of His grace."* Ephesians 1:7 NKJV

9. <u>He Promises That Nothing Can Separate Us from Him:</u> *"For I am persuaded that neither death nor life, nor angels, nor principalities, nor powers, nor things present nor things to come, nor height nor depth, nor any other created thing, shall be able to separate us from the love of God which is in Christ Jesus our Lord."* Romans 8:38-39 NKJV

10. <u>He Promises Eternal Life to All Who Believe in Him:</u> *"And as Moses lifted up the serpent in the wilderness, even so must the Son of Man be lifted up, that whoever believes in Him should not perish but have eternal life. For God so loved the world that He gave His only begotten Son, that whoever believes in Him should not perish but have everlasting life."* John 3:14-16 NKJV

Hope Through Hard Times

God's promises also include that we will have trials and tribulations while we are here on earth (John 16:33). We will suffer in this broken world, but we have what the world does not have, which is hope. It is hope that comes from our Heavenly Father, His Son and our Savior Jesus Christ, and our Helper the Holy Spirit. It is with this eternal hope that we can endure trials. It allows us to move forward with the certainty and confidence that God is sovereign and in control. He will provide the strength to persevere and endure, even when we can't see the finish line. Yes, there will be moments of despair, but God also provides us with assurances that give us hope and encouragement as we are in the midst of our suffering.

God gives us the assurance that He uses our trials to serve a purpose in our lives. It is through trials that our faith is tested and strengthened. He uses them to refine us and build our character. A common but true statement is that "God cares more about our character than our comfort." When we endure our trials to the end it shows that our faith is true, and without true faith we have no real hope. It is through trials that we learn to persevere and remain steadfast in our hope (James 1: 2-4).

God gives us the assurance that He will bring an end to our trials (1 Peter 1:6). It may sometimes feel like a trial is never going to end, and unfortunately there is no timeline given to us. Psalm 30:5b NKJV promises, *"...Weeping may endure for a night, But joy comes in the morning."* The night might last for months or years, but the morning will come. Sometimes death is what brings an end to the suffering, but we need to remember that death is not permanent for those who love the Lord. He has given us the gift of eternal life and we have the hope that we will be reunited again in His kingdom.

As I wrote this chapter our trial of many years ended on June 30, 2023, when the Lord took our daughter home to be healed and restored. Our daughter struggled with mental illness and lived in anguish for many years, but even in her illness she always had a heart for God. There have been some very dark nights over the years, but our weeping will be turned into joy when we see our daughter in heaven as the beautiful woman God created. That is our hope and certainty.

This leads to the next assurance, which is that God will comfort us in our pain (2 Corinthians 1:3-4). God promises to remain close to us in our suffering and draws near when we are broken-hearted. We have a compassionate Savior in Jesus, because He understands our suffering and knows our heartaches. He personally understands the pain we are going through and can bring healing to our souls. *"He heals the brokenhearted and binds up their wounds"* (Psalms 147:3 NKJV).

God also gives us the assurance that He hears our prayers and is aware of our hardships (Isaiah 59:1). He hears our cries and sees our sufferings, and when we have no words left to pray the Holy Spirit speaks for us (Romans 8:26-27). We have the assurance that even when we are at a loss for words, He knows our pain and needs. He wraps His loving arms around us and whispers "I've got you."

Finally, we have the assurance that God has overcome the world and has won the war. Jesus conquered death when He went to the cross. When we feel like our hope is fading and that we are losing the battle, we need to look to the cross and remember Jesus is our victory. We are in a spiritual battle and Satan wants to steal our hope. We are reminded in Ephesians 6:12 NKJV, *"For we do not wrestle against flesh and blood, but against principalities, against powers, against the rulers of the darkness of this age, against spiritual hosts of wickedness in the heavenly places."* God has given us His armor to fight against the enemy. Ephesians 6:13-18 instructs us to:

- Gird our waist with truth
- Put on the breastplate of righteousness
- Shod our feet with the gospel of peace
- Take up the shield of faith
- Put on the helmet of salvation
- Take up the sword of the Spirit
- Pray always, be watchful, and persevere

God has instructed us that when we go through times of suffering, we are to put our trust and hope in Him. We are His children and have the power of God within us to fight the enemy (1 John 4:4). Don't allow yourself to give into despair and instead focus on the assurance that His promises are true. Our hope is founded on the certainty that God has given us the victory.

Hope for the Future

> *"For I know the thoughts that I think toward you, says the Lord, thoughts of peace and not of evil, to give you a future and a hope."* Jeremiah 29:11 NKJV

We live in this world but are not of this world. Where the world views a future full of despair, fear, and hopelessness, our view is grounded in the truth that God has promised us a future and a hope. He is our rock, our hope, our joy, our salvation and our protector (Psalm 62: 5-6).

Our future hope is not based on earthly riches and power, but on the promise that we will have inner, immovable peace, and unending joy as we persevere through trials (James 1:12). We have a God who richly blesses us with His eternal heavenly blessings as we remain faithful and obedient.

Finally, and most of all, our future hope is solidified in the promise that Jesus is returning again. He will restore the world under His reign, and all will be made just and right. There will be no more sickness or sorrow. God tells us in Revelation 21:4, NKJV, *"And God will wipe away every tear from their eyes; there shall be no more death, nor sorrow, nor crying. There shall be no more pain, for the former things have passed away."*

In the meantime, as we wait for His return, we are to continue serving the Lord. Read Matthew 25:34-40. He knows our labor as we care for those who need us. He tells us that when we care for the sick, poor, and downcast, we are caring for Him. We are His messengers of love and hope, and God sees us as we care for our loved ones. Rest in His promises and hold on to the eternal hope that someday we will all be healed and restored when we enter His Kingdom.

Reflection and Application

1. What is your hope as you care for your loved one? Is your hope based on wishful thinking or on the promises of God?

_____

_____

_____

_____

2. Do any of the listed promises of God bring you hope and comfort? If so, which ones?

_____

_____

_____

_____

3. Do any of God's assurances encourage you as you maintain hope during hard times? Which ones?

_____

_____

_____

_____

4. What is your future hope? What promises in God's word give you hope for the future? How can you apply them as you are caring for your loved one?

_____

_____

_____

_____

Notes and Journaling

CHAPTER 14

Advocating for Our Loved Ones

Mental Illness with School Age Children

Mental Illness has dramatically increased among our children and youth. There may be a variety of factors that have contributed to this increase, including the breakdown of the family unit, divorce and/or single parenting, societal pressures, social media, and the aftermath of the Covid pandemic. According to the American Psychological Association's 2023 Trends Report, *"The COVID-19 pandemic era ushered in a new set of challenges for youth in the United States, leading to a mental health crisis as declared by the United States surgeon general just over a year ago."*

The American Academy of Child & Adolescent Psychiatry (www.aacap.org) lists signs and symptoms that may indicate your child is suffering from mental illness:

- School problems and/or drop in grades
- Frequent fighting with peers, authority figures, and/or members of their family
- Trouble sleeping
- Feeling sad
- Thoughts about suicide or running away

- Excessive weight loss or gain
- Troubling or disturbing thoughts
- Use of drugs or alcohol
- Withdrawal or isolation from friends and/or family members
- Injuring or killing animals
- Stealing or lying
- Mood swings
- Setting fires
- Obsessive thoughts or compulsive behaviors
- Dangerous or self-destructive behavior
- Trouble paying attention
- Anxiety or frequent worries

Facing the reality of having a loved one with mental illness can be overwhelming for families. The first hurdle is recognizing and accepting that your loved one has a mental illness. The next hurdle is accessing the care and services your loved one needs. Oftentimes mental health professionals have long wait lists, sometimes months long, before they can even be assessed. Health insurance plans can also delay their care or provide limited coverage. The schools may not understand or be supportive of a child's needs. All these factors force families to become advocates for the loved one.

Advocating for School Age Children and Youth

As parents or guardians of a school age child, you are their best advocate for getting them the care they need. It may begin with just getting them seen by a healthcare provider and/or mental health professional. You may have to make repeated phone calls or go up the chain of command to get them seen. You may have to be the "squeaky wheel" that keeps calling to check if there has been a cancellation in the schedule. You may have to research for a different provider who can see your child sooner. You may also need to pursue getting a second opinion regarding your child's diagnosis and treatment plan. All these challenges are time consuming and stressful. To help alleviate some of the burden and stress, parents/guardians may need to "divide and conquer." It is important to discuss the issues with each other and divide the responsibilities to get the results you need. Recognize each other's strengths and assign responsibilities according to your strengths.

As the parent/guardian you may also need to be an advocate for your child within the school system and in the classroom. You are your child's best educational advocate, especially when they are too young to speak for themselves. It is important to research and learn about your child's rights to obtain the resources your child needs to be successful at school.

One of the rights that parents have is what is referred to as "FAPE," which is an acronym that means every child has a right to a Free Appropriate Public Education. This is a federal law that gives rights under the Individuals with Disabilities Education Act (IDEA). In California this falls under California's Education Code. What this means is that your child's education (in public schools) must be at no cost to the parent, must provide programs or services that meet your child's unique needs, must provide the same rights to attend public schools as all children, and must guarantee that students with disabilities receive related services. Meeting your child's needs can range from implementing simple accommodations in the classroom, to requiring more specialized services for them to be successful at school. You also have the right to meet with the school administrator, counselor, and teacher(s) to discuss your child's needs.

If it is determined that your child may require Special Education services, then the school needs to begin the IEP (Individualized Education Plan) process. An IEP is a written, legal document that is designed to meet a child's individual needs. It includes assessments, goals, classroom accommodations, and district services that will be specifically provided for your child. As a parent you have the right to request that your child be assessed for an IEP to determine if they meet the criteria for receiving IEP services. You may have to put your request in writing or obtain a note from your child's healthcare provider. If your child does not meet the criteria for having an IEP, the alternative is a 504 Plan. A 504 Plan is also a legal document that provides mandated accommodations for your child at school and in the classroom. The 504 plan differs from an IEP in that the 504 Plan does not include assessments, goals or district services. Both the IEP and 504 Plan require yearly meetings with the parents, administrator, counselor, and teachers to review the plan and make changes if needed.

Below are some tips to help you advocate for your child within the school and educational system:

1. Educate yourself about your child's diagnosis and needs. This can include reading literature, watching educational videos, or attending workshops. Explore your child's strengths and weaknesses so that you can work with the school to figure out how to best support their needs.

2. Keep all your paperwork organized into files. This includes report cards, progress reports, IEP's or 504 Plans, and samples of their classwork and test scores. This information is valuable in helping to provide the best interventions for your child's educational success.

3. Build relationships with school personnel. This includes the teacher, administrator, counselor, and service providers (school psychologist, speech therapist, mental health resource specialist, and any other providers who work with your child). Keeping communication open can prevent misunderstandings and provide early interventions when issues arise.

4. Don't be hesitant to ask questions. It is important that you understand and agree to your child's services, goals, and accommodations before you give your consent to the services. It would help to write down any questions you have beforehand and during the meeting so that you can get your questions answered. You have the right to ask for further assessments and additional services if you are not comfortable with what is being offered to your child. You can also hire an IEP advocate if you feel you are not making progress with getting your child's needs met.

5. Control your emotions and stay calm. The school staff wants to support you and your child, even if you disagree with them. Allowing your emotions to take over is unproductive

and can create tension with the Team members. It is understandable that you want to protect your child, and because of this it can be easy to become emotional. Consider bringing a friend or family member who can help you stay focused and remain calm.

6. Remember that you are an equal member of the decision-making Team. Don't allow yourself to feel pressured by the school staff to make decisions. It is important to listen to the staff's input and suggestions, but don't feel you have to agree with them. Ultimately, you know what is best for your child.

7. Learn about your child's rights. Every child has the right to a Free and Appropriate Public Education (FAPE), which falls under the Individuals with Disabilities Education Act (IDEA). If your child qualifies for specialized services, they have the right to classroom accommodations such as extended time on tests or preferred seating. Be informed about the school's legal requirement to assess your child and provide services if they qualify.

8. Talk to your child. Ask your child about how they are doing at school. Does your child know what accommodations they are entitled to and is the teacher providing them? It is important to make sure the plan and services are being implemented. Teach your child to speak up for themselves and to learn to self-advocate.

9. Learn the terms and acronyms. It can be confusing when school staff talk to you using common lingo among school personnel. If you don't understand what is being said, ask them to clarify. Write it down to help you learn and remember for next time.

10. Communicate regularly. IEP and 504 Plan meetings are held yearly and provide input from staff on your child's needs and progress. But in addition to the yearly meetings, it is important to get input about your child's performance throughout the school year. Check in with the teacher regularly and ask for updates on how your child is doing. Ask how you can provide additional support at home. This will allow you to intervene early if an issue is beginning to develop. It also keeps you informed of your child's progress and identifies where they need help.

Advocating for Adults

Advocating for adult family members can be challenging. Even though we see that they are having difficulty managing their lives and need support, there is little we can do unless they agree to our help. If they are willing to discuss their challenges, it may be helpful to prepare ahead of time and write down how you can help advocate for them. Let them see that they are still in control and will make decisions. Your role will be to support them and be a voice for them. Communicate that you want to be there to help them overcome obstacles and help deal with the bureaucracy of government agencies and insurance companies. It may take time and baby steps for them to trust you. Be patient and back away if they are feeling threatened by your involvement. You can approach them again at a later time when they are calmer and in a better state of mind.

There are times when your adult loved one is incapable of making healthy decisions for themselves. This is especially hard when they are refusing treatment or don't want help. Below are some tips and/or strategies you can use when talking with them about getting the care that they need.

- Explain: Share your concerns with your loved one and explain why you are worried about them. Stay focused on their present behavior and not their diagnosis. For example, you might say, "I'm worried because I've noticed that you seem more anxious and not sleeping these past few weeks."

- Listen: Ask questions about how your loved one feels about treatment and listen to their response. Ask them to explain to you why they do not want help and listen without reacting.

- Encourage communication: Ask them how you can support them. Give them the opportunity to tell you how you can be most helpful. Be open to their input. Their requests may be small at first, but they may gradually work up to asking for other forms of help.

- Provide options: Offer suggestions on ways that you can support them. For example, offer to help them find a therapist, psychiatrist, or support group. They may be relieved and welcome your help. Make sure to give them choices and options.

- Remain open: If they continue to refuse to get help, it's normal to want to stop offering assistance. Continue to keep an open dialogue with your loved one. Keep the door open to discuss getting treatment at a later time. Respect their boundaries and continue to remind them that you are there to support them.

God's Word About Advocacy

Proverbs 31:8-9 NIV states, *"Speak up for those who cannot speak for themselves, for the rights of all who are destitute. Speak up and judge fairly; defend the rights of the poor and needy."* As believers in Christ, we are called to speak up for those who cannot or are unable to speak for themselves. Proverbs 31:8-9 clearly tells us to stand up for those who are defenseless and defend their rights. We need to push away fears, insecurities, or whatever keeps us silent. We are to stand up and be the voice for the voiceless.

God's word provides guidance with how we are to advocate for others:

- First, we need to seek God and listen. We must listen to His counsel, listen to the Holy Spirit's leading, study His word, and be obedient to His commands.

- Next, we need to pray. We need to prayerfully examine our hearts and allow God to reveal to us reasons we have not spoken up for our loved one. We need to ask God for His courage to speak up, and His wisdom to know how and when we should speak. Allow Him to use the gifts and tools He has already given us.

- Lastly, we are to take action. We are to do what He tells us and put His words into action. We are called to love and to seek justice for those in need. He wants us to be an advocate for our loved ones and to be their voice.

Scriptures Regarding Advocacy:

"Defend the poor and fatherless; Do justice to the afflicted and needy. Deliver the poor and needy; Free them from the hand of the wicked." Psalms 82:3-4 NKJV

"Bear one another's burdens, and so fulfill the law of Christ." Galatians 6:2 NKJV

"And let us not grow weary while doing good, for in due season we shall reap if we do not lose heart." Galatians 6:9 NKJV

"Let each of you look out not only for his own interests, but also for the interests of others." Philippians 2:4 NKJV

Reflection and Application

1. What challenges or obstacles have you experienced with trying to get care for your loved one?

_____

_____

_____

_____

2. In your own words, describe what being an advocate means to you. Are there any issues or obstacles keeping you from being an advocate for your loved one?

_____

_____

_____

_____

3. Have you ever had to be an advocate for your child, adult child, or adult loved one? What situations did you have to advocate for? What were the outcomes?

_____

_____

_____

_____

4. Are there issues with an adult loved one refusing to get help? How has it affected you and/or your family?

_____

_____

_____

_____

Notes and Journaling

CHAPTER 15

Challenges When Caring for Adult Loved Ones

Impact on the Family

Families who are caring for an adult with mental illness face difficult challenges when providing support and care for their loved one. Adult loved ones can include parents, spouses, siblings, adult children, and children of mentally ill adults. The onset of mental illness usually occurs during adolescence or young adulthood, and it can impact the person's developmental process. As a result, family functioning and relationships can be stressed. Family members often feel responsible for their loved one's illness. There may even be situations where the family is held responsible for their loved one's actions, and it's not uncommon for legal and social service systems to be involved. The burden of their care can be significant and may last for a lifetime for family members who stay committed.

Dealing with an adult family member who is mentally ill can create a multitude of feelings for family members. For example, the family may feel ill-equipped to deal with the mental illness or may feel overwhelmed when trying to help their loved one manage their daily responsibilities. The family may feel guilt or blame for not dealing with the illness earlier. Feelings of frustration are also common because the family has no control over their treatment. Siblings may worry that they or their children will develop a mental illness, or worry about their own future and the impact their sibling's illness will have on their own immediate family members. These feelings and concerns are normal for families with a mentally ill adult. To help manage these feelings it is important for family members to communicate with each other and be open about their concerns. Together they should set a plan for how they will or will not support their mentally ill loved one. It is also important that boundaries are established and agreed upon among the family members.

Helping Adult Loved Ones

There are a few practical things you can do when trying to help your adult loved one. The first step is to educate yourself about your loved one's illness, so you are informed and better prepared. To better help your loved one, you need knowledge about their diagnosis, symptoms, and recommended treatments. Spend time researching information from reliable resources. NAMI (National Alliance on Mental Illness) is an excellent resource that can provide you with information. You can also attend conferences or trainings about mental illness to gain information from other individuals who are dealing with similar situations. Participating in a support group for loved ones with mental illness can also help you to gain insight and obtain support from others. Gaining knowledge about the illness will help you better understand why your loved one is behaving the way they are, and will help give you a sense of control and insight over the situation.

In addition to knowledge, it is helpful to develop an empathetic attitude when approaching your mentally ill loved one. Try putting yourself mentally in their shoes to understand what they are going through. Learn how their brain processes information. Be empathetic towards how they are feeling and what they are dealing with. Focus on their positive qualities and recognize the improvements they have made. Encourage their efforts and remember to practice patience and be prepared for setbacks.

It is also important to learn how to communicate with your loved one in a positive way. This can be accomplished by putting the focus on your feelings and concerns instead of on their behavior. Instead of saying "you" say "I." For example, instead of saying "you're irresponsible when you don't show up for work", you can say "I am worried that you will lose your job if you don't show up to work." Putting the focus on your feelings instead of their actions can make them less likely to react defensively or negatively. This positive dialogue will hopefully open a conversation where they won't feel threatened and may be more open to your suggestions.

Encouraging Your Loved One to Get Help

Convincing a mentally ill loved one to get help is one of the biggest challenges that families can face. Mental illness recovery frequently includes periods of instability or setbacks. It is often when symptoms exacerbate that the person becomes increasingly resistant to getting treatment. This can create tension and frustration within the family.

When your loved one is refusing treatment, it may help if you objectively ask them why. Listen and try to stay neutral. They may have valid reasons for not wanting treatment. For example, they may refuse to take the medication because of unpleasant side effects, or they feel it didn't help. They may also feel that they can manage their symptoms without medication. They may have had a bad experience with therapy or didn't like the therapist. Allow them to share their feelings and experiences regarding past treatments. If they know you are listening, they may be more willing to discuss other treatment options. Encourage them to see how with help and the right treatment they can achieve their life goals. You may need to have an honest discussion about how their illness is affecting your relationship with them. Be clear about your expectations and the possible outcomes if they agree or disagree with getting treatment. Discuss with them what the positive outcomes could be versus the potential consequences of their decisions. Be prepared to follow through with the consequences.

Another factor that may keep your loved one from getting treatment may be that they are feeling overwhelmed with the obstacles they have to face to access the treatment. This can include finding a treatment program, scheduling appointments, dealing with insurance, or managing transportation. Let them know if you are available to help them and willing to work with them. If you have limitations, be sure to clarify them. Write out a plan with your loved one and clearly state how and in what ways you will help them.

In some cases, your loved one may not be able to recognize that they have a mental illness. It may not just be denial, but another medical condition called "anosognosia." This is when the person is mentally unable to understand they have a mental illness, and as a result they refuse treatment. If their refusal causes a significant worsening of symptoms, it could lead to a crisis situation. Examples of worsening symptoms include:

- They are increasingly isolating themselves
- They are having trouble sleeping or eating
- There is an increase with drinking or drug use
- They are unable to communicate or concentrate
- They appear distant or have a vacant expression
- They make statements that seem strange or don't make sense (e.g., they believe someone is watching them, or they hear messages over the air waves).
- They are hearing voices or seeing things that you don't

If your loved one is having serious symptoms that may involve them hurting themselves or someone else, then it becomes an urgent matter and you need to call for support immediately. The police department has a Psychiatric Emergency Response Team (PERT) that can assist with a mental health crisis or mental illness related emergency. The goal of the PERT team is to de-escalate crisis situations and provide appropriate referrals. The PERT Team can be accessed through the 9-1-1 emergency system.

Where is God in All This?

Sometimes, in our darkest moments, we wonder where God is. We ask ourselves, "why is He allowing this to happen?" or "why won't He heal my loved one?" It is in those times that we need to remember that God has not forsaken us, and He promises that He never will us. He tells us in Hebrews 13:5 NKJV, *"…I will never leave you nor forsake you."* Even though we may not understand what God is doing, we are told to trust that He is in control because He is sovereign. God is all powerful, all knowing, governs all and is over-all.

In this broken world we cannot stop disease and sickness from happening. It is not your fault that your loved one is mentally ill. It is not something you could have stopped or prevented. Mankind has brought this on themselves through sin and rebellion. But the good news is that God has not abandoned us. He is with us in our pain and provides us the way to endure it.

Below are some steps you can apply to help both you and your loved one continue to endure:

1. Take time to understand. As parents or caregivers, we want to help and guide our loved ones, but their illness can put up a roadblock. They have lost control over their own thoughts and may just want you to understand. Take time to listen to them without judgement and empathize with them. This may not be the time to take action, but instead be a time of listening and understanding.

2. Remind them of your love. As parents, our love does not fade as our child becomes an adult. This is also true with a mentally ill adult child. If anything, our love drives us to try to want to make them better so they can be happy. They may not realize how much you love them, and may even believe you stopped loving them because of their illness. Remind them daily of your love for them, and that you love them just as much today as the day they were born. They need to hear it, even if they act like they don't believe it.

3. Recognize that even as the parent you may not be the best person to help your adult child. If there is constant tension, frustration, and conflict you may need to step back and reevaluate your situation. Seek help from someone you both trust who can provide the care you need. It does not mean you are a failure. It is recognizing that both you and your loved one need additional support.

4. Ask your loved what they want to do to feel better. As an adult they have the authority to make their own decisions. Forcing decisions or treatment on them will most likely lead to conflict. When they are asked instead of being told, they may be more receptive to your input. It allows them to feel in control.

5. It is okay to set limits. It is important to set boundaries with your loved one, especially if they are mistreating you. You have the right to be safe in your own home. Setting boundaries means you are taking care of yourself and showing yourself love and respect.

6. Don't do this alone, get help. First spend time in prayer with God. He is always present and listening, even when we don't feel Him. Next seek help from a professional. This can be a therapist, church leader, or physician. It helps to talk to someone who can provide solid counsel. It doesn't mean you are weak. It is recognizing that you are in a very difficult situation and need support.

Promises in God's Word

"The Lord is near to those who have a broken heart, and saves such as have a contrite spirit. Many are the afflictions of the righteous, But the Lord delivers him out of them all." Psalms 34:18-19 NKJV

"My flesh and my heart fail; But God is the strength of my heart and my portion forever." Psalms 73:26 NKJV

"Come to Me, all you who labor and are heavy laden, and I will give you rest." Matthew 11:28 NKJV

Reflection and Application

1. How has your family been impacted by your mentally ill adult loved one? What are some of the feelings or frustrations you are experiencing as you deal with them?

_____

_____

_____

_____

2. What challenges have you faced as you've dealt with your mentally ill adult loved one? Write out your challenges even if your loved one is not an adult.

_____

_____

_____

_____

3. What strategies have you used to support your loved one with getting treatment? Have they been successful? Why or why not?

_____

_____

_____

_____

4. Of the steps that were listed to help you endure as you try to care for your loved, which of them can you apply to your situation?

_____

_____

_____

_____

Notes and Journaling

CHAPTER 16

Helping Your Loved One with Life Skills

One of the many challenges that the mentally ill face is learning how to manage life skills. These life skills can range from managing their basic physical needs, to learning how to control their emotions, health, finances, relationships, job or school performance. Our goal as caregivers is to guide and support them with mastering these skills so they can become independent and better at managing their mental illness.

Basic Life Skills

Developing life skills may need to begin with them learning how to manage their basic, physical needs. With severe mental illness the person may not be able to adequately take care of their physical needs. These needs can include:

Sleep: Getting enough sleep is essential for health. Lack of sleep can lead to increased anxiety or depression. It can make symptoms of the mental illness worse or possibly trigger mania, psychosis, or paranoia. The amount of recommended sleep is 8-9 hours a night. Learning to have a healthy sleep cycle is important in being able to function in daily life. If sleep is a significant issue with your loved one, then you should consider consulting with their healthcare provider for possible medical interventions.

Nutrition: Good nutrition is important for both mental and physical health. Poor nutrition can cause lethargy, fatigue, impaired decision making, and possibly lead to depression. Processed foods are one of the worst sources of nutrition because they primarily consist of high sugar, high fat, and refined flour. Understanding the importance of good nutrition and having a diet that includes fruits and vegetables, lean proteins, low fat dairy and whole grains will improve overall health. Have your loved one help with planning and preparing meals. Teach them which foods are better for their health and which are not. Show them how to shop for nutritious foods, such as focusing on the produce, meat, dairy, and bread sections of the grocery store. Teach them how to read labels and understand what they mean. You may even need to educate yourself with understanding and interpreting labels. Good nutrition is important for everyone in the family.

Exercise: Being physically active benefits both physical and mental health. Exercise improves your mood by causing the brain to release "feel good" chemicals such as endorphins and serotonin. It reduces stress and anxiety, helps improve sleep, and improves mental alertness. Exercise is also a good coping strategy to use when you are feeling overwhelmed and stressed. Create an exercise plan together with your loved one that will benefit both of you. Start small such as taking a short walk 3-4 times a week. Explore what types of activities interest you and your loved one (can be different), and plan how you will incorporate them into your daily lives.

Personal Self-Care: Sometimes basic hygiene practices are neglected by your loved one. Teaching the importance of bathing, brushing teeth, shaving, combing hair, and hand washing can be a challenge. With mental illness, poor hygiene is one of the signs that symptoms are worsening. You may need to start with just one skill, such as just brushing their teeth. Once this becomes routine for them, then add on another skill. Hopefully over time hygiene practices will become part of their daily routine.

Higher Level Life Skills

If your loved one is managing their basic life skills, then move towards the more challenging ones. Some higher-level skills can include managing medical care/treatment plans (including medication), domestic tasks, finances, social skills, and job or school performance. As you address these areas, it is important to break down each skill into smaller steps. They may need to master one step at a time to be able to manage the whole skill.

Medical Care: Teaching your loved one to manage their medical care may need to start with them understanding and accepting their illness. They may be in denial about their diagnosis. Work with their healthcare provider to help explain their illness so they realize that they need treatment just like any other medical diagnosis. Use examples with them such as Diabetes needing insulin, or asthma needing inhalers.

The next step is helping them manage their treatment plan. If they are being treated with medication help them to be organized and consistent. This can include using a pill box to help them remember to take the medication. You may need to show them how to use the pill box and how to fill it each week (especially if they take medication more than once a day). Teach them to monitor how many pills they have left, and how to reorder or set up a plan that automatically does refills.

Your loved one may also need help with learning how to manage their appointments. Help them with setting up a calendar for their appointments, which can be done electronically or with a calendar appointment book (whichever they prefer). You may need to prompt them to remember to record their appointments and check the schedule daily. Over time it will hopefully become routine for them to manage their calendar and appointments.

Domestic Tasks: Depending on the severity of your loved one's illness, they may need help with cooking and preparing meals, washing dishes, cleaning up after themselves, and/or doing laundry. Don't try to conquer these tasks all at once. Allow your loved one to choose which task they want to work on first and start with baby steps. For example, with learning how to prepare meals you may want to start first with making a list of what ingredients are needed, and then go to the store to shop for the ingredients. Start with simple meals and encourage healthy choices. Work with them as they cook the meals and help them with using a timer and selecting the correct cookware and temperatures. Teach them to read directions on the packages or recipes. It may take several meals before they become competent with mastering this skill.

Maintenance: Another common challenge is their ability to keep up with laundry and maintain a clean environment. One of the biggest hurdles is getting them to keep a routine so these tasks don't mount up to a huge undertaking. Work with them to create a weekly schedule where they can set aside a day and time to accomplish these tasks. Help them to understand that staying on top of these tasks will keep them from feeling overwhelmed. As your loved one gains confidence with managing one domestic skill, then decide with them which skill they will work on next. You may have to go back from time to time to reinforce a previous skill that they had already accomplished. Be prepared for setbacks.

Finances: Managing finances is much more challenging and is even difficult for people without mental illness. The first step with helping your loved one to manage their finances is to show them how to set their priorities to understand where they need to spend their money first. Explain to them that rent, utilities, cell phone, and food are their first priority when it comes to spending their income. Help them to understand that their total spending needs to match their income to make it financially to the end of each month. This also includes teaching them to understand bank accounts and learn how to manage their checking account. Many people no longer keep written checkbook records and prefer to check their account online for the balance. The problem is that oftentimes their expenditure has not cleared through the bank yet and they have less than they think. Encourage them to keep a record and/or their receipts so they remember their spending. Create a budget with them to help them balance their income and spending.

Social Skills: People who struggle with mental illness often have difficulty interacting or connecting with other people. Poor social skills can negatively impact many areas of their lives including work/school, family, relationships, or interacting within the community. Having difficulty with social skills is not the same as simply not being social. They may want to interact, but when they do it doesn't go well. Their conversation may come across as being strange or odd, or their behaviors may be misunderstood. They may also have difficulty picking up on social cues or understanding social rules. They may struggle with controlling their emotions.

Teaching social skills is not easy, and you may need to start with helping your loved one see or understand how they present themselves to other people. A common challenge is the ability to maintain eye contact. They may feel insecure or threatened when they have extended eye contact with another person. Practice with them having a conversation and maintaining eye contact. You may have to start with 15 second segments of maintaining eye contact and gradually build from there.

Another skill is learning how to manage their emotions. Role play and practice with them situations where they might become upset. Rehearse with them ways they can manage their emotions. You can also use videos to show examples of appropriate or inappropriate behaviors. Discuss with your loved one the different behaviors and reinforce the good ones. You may also need to teach them how to have a phone conversation, which can be difficult because they can't see the person to see their social cues. Remember it is going to take time and practice for them to understand and improve their social skills. Be patient and use opportunities to teach them.

Work or School Management: Demands at work or school can create stress and exacerbate mental illness symptoms. Oftentimes when the mentally ill person is experiencing an increase in symptoms, it will impact their job/school attendance and performance. It is important to help your loved one be proactive and assist them with communicating with their employer or school administrator about their illness. All information that is shared with them is required to be kept confidential. Remind your loved one that providing information will help their workplace or school understand their illness so they can provide appropriate accommodations.

As an employee, your mentally ill loved one is protected under the "Americans with Disabilities Act" (ADA), where employers are required to "provide reasonable accommodation to qualified individuals with disabilities." At school your loved one may qualify for support services and accommodations to help them to be successful. Work with your loved one and guide them with learning how to access and utilize the services available to them. Help them to know what accommodations to ask for (e.g. a quiet workspace, allowed to listen to music, take frequent 1-2 minute breaks, etc.). It would also help to practice stress reducing exercises with them to help them manage stress at work or school. Plan strategies ahead of time so they are ready to implement them when they are feeling anxious or overwhelmed. Teaching them to communicate their needs and to be prepared for stressful situations will help them achieve success.

Supporting Spiritual Development

Studies have proven repeatedly that faith plays an important role in improving the symptoms and quality of life of those suffering with mental illness. Researchers at the Mayo Clinic stated, *"Most studies have shown that religious involvement and spirituality are associated with better health outcomes, including greater longevity, coping skills, and health-related quality of life (even during terminal illness) and less anxiety, depression, and suicide. Several studies have shown that addressing the spiritual needs of the patient may enhance recovery from illness." (https://www.mayoclinicproceedings. org/article/S0025-6196(11)62799-7/pdf)*

As family and/or caregivers of mentally ill loved ones, we play an important role with guiding them in their faith and helping them to understand where God is in their illness. Explain to your loved one that mental illness has been present since the fall of man. Show them Biblical characters who struggled with forms of mental illness and how God met their needs.

Elijah struggled with depression and despair after his confrontation with the Baal priests and wanted to die (read 1 Kings 18:20–19:12). But God sent an angel to him to comfort him and give him food and water. Then God personally came to him and showed Elijah that He does not come to us in windstorms, earthquakes, or fire. He comes to us speaking in a still small voice. He whispers His encouragement to us.

King David had multiple accounts of depression and despair throughout his life. He poured out his heart through the Psalms and cried out in his despair. But each time he was filled with sadness, he then experienced the hope and joy he received from God. His faith never wavered, even during his darkest moments. He always returned to God and loved Him with all his heart, soul, mind, and strength.

Job went into a severe depression and despair when he lost everything. He was a wealthy and blessed man who feared God and turned from evil. God allowed Satan to test Job and he lost everything. His children, health, livestock, crops, servants, everything except his wife. Job went into a severe depression but remained faithful to God. He never stopped trusting God, and God richly blessed him beyond everything he lost.

Paul struggled with despair during his long imprisonment in Rome, but he never lost his faith and remained focused on his ministry. He wrote letters during that time to teach and encourage new Christians, and those letters make up the majority of the New Testament that continue to teach us to this day. Throughout his ministry he experienced multiple hardships and persecution, but he never stopped praising God in his suffering.

Share these examples and more with your loved one to show them how God can greatly use them even in their mental health struggles. God is faithful, and even though we walk through storms in this life, He promises to protect us. He will not allow us to fall victim to the storms, but instead helps us to be overcomers. Share with your loved one the below steps to help them trust God with their illness.

- Rest on His promises: God promises hope and freedom as you learn to live with mental illness. God has always cared for you and will continue to care for you, even in the midst of your illness.

- <u>Remember He is always with you:</u> God promises that even when you are in your darkest moments, not wanting to go on, He is with you. He walks you through the storms and helps you to face things that seem impossible to overcome. He has already won the victory over all your struggles and trials.
- <u>Read His Scripture:</u> Read the Bible and cling to His promises. Memorize verses that bring you hope and comfort. Pray about how you can apply His Word to your life.
- <u>Pray:</u> Spend time in prayer and realize that you have a God who listens, cares, and loves you unconditionally.

Application and Reflection

1. Does your loved one have challenges with some Life Skills? If so, which one's concern you? What steps can you take to teach or help them with managing those Life Skills?

_____

_____

_____

_____

_____

2. How do you feel about people in the Bible who struggled with mental illness? How does their example and God's comfort encourage you?

_____

_____

_____

_____

_____

3. What steps can you implement to help your loved one in their faith as they struggle with their illness? Are they open to discussing their faith? How can we as a group pray for you and your loved one?

_____

_____

_____

_____

_____

Notes and Journaling

Printed in the United States
by Baker & Taylor Publisher Services

Printed in the United States
by Baker & Taylor Publisher Services